CW00684261

Procopius History of the Wars, Books V. and VI.

by Procopius

ISBN: 9781318854622

HardPress
8345 NW 66TH ST #2561
MIAMI FL 33166-2626
USA
Email: info@hardpress.net

Ordering Information:

Quantity sales. Special discounts are available on quantity purchases by corporations, associations, and others. For details, contact the publisher by email at the address above.

Printed in the United States of America, United Kingdom and Australia

PROCOPIUS

WITH AN ENGLISH TRANSLATION BY

H.B. DEWING

IN SEVEN VOLUMES

III

HISTORY OF THE WARS, BOOKS V AND VI

LONDON

WILLIAM HEINEMANN LTD

CAMBRIDGE, MASSACHUSETTS

HARVARD UNIVERSITY PRESS

First printed 1919

Printed in Great Britain

CONTENTS

---

[1]

PROCOPIUS OF CAESAREA

HISTORY OF THE WARS:

BOOK V

THE GOTHIC WAR

[3]

PROCOPIUS OF CAESAREA

HISTORY OF THE WARS: BOOK V

THE GOTHIC WAR

I

Such, then, were the fortunes of the Romans in Libya. I shall now proceed to the Gothic War, first telling all that befell the Goths and Italians before this war.

474-491 A.D. During the reign of Zeno Byzantium the power in the West was held by Augustus, whom the Romans used to call by the diminutive name Augustulus because he took over the empire while still a lad, July 31, 475 A.D. his father Orestes, a man of the greatest discretion, administering it as regent for him. Now it happened that the Romans a short time before had induced the Sciri and Alani and certain other Gothic nations to form an alliance with them; and from that time on it was their fortune to suffer at the hand of Alaric and Attila those things which have been told in the previous narrative.[1] And in proportion as the barbarian element among them became strong, just so did the prestige of the Roman soldiers forthwith decline, and under the fair name of alliance [5]they were more and more tyrannized over by the intruders and oppressed by them; so that the barbarians ruthlessly forced many other measures upon the Romans much against their will and finally demanded that they should divide with them the entire land of Italy. And indeed they commanded Orestes to give them the third part of this, and when he would by no means agree to do so, they killed him immediately. July 28, 476 A.D. Now there was a certain man among the Romans named Odoacer, one of the bodyguards of the emperor, and he at that time agreed to carry out their commands, on condition that they should set him upon the throne. And when he had received the supreme power in this way, July 28, 476 A.D. he did the emperor no further harm, but allowed him to live thenceforth as a private citizen. And by giving the third part of the land to the barbarians, and in this way gaining their allegiance most firmly, he held the supreme power securely for ten years.[2]

It was at about this same time that the Goths also, who were dwelling in Thrace with the permission of the emperor, took up arms against the Romans under the leadership of Theoderic, a man who was of patrician rank and had attained the consular office in Byzantium. But the Emperor Zeno, who understood how to settle to his advantage any situation in which he found himself, advised Theoderic to proceed to Italy, attack Odoacer, and win for himself and the Goths the western dominion. For it was better for him, he said, especially as he had attained the senatorial dignity, to force out a usurper and be ruler [7]over all the Romans and Italians than to incur the great risk of a decisive struggle with the emperor.

Now Theoderic was pleased with the suggestion and went to Italy, and he was followed by the Gothic host, who placed in their waggons the women and children and such of their chattels as they were able to take with them. And when they came near the Ionian Gulf,[3] they were quite unable to cross over it, since they had no ships at hand; and so they made the journey around the gulf, advancing through the land of the Taulantii and the other nations of that region. Here the forces of Odoacer encountered them, but after being defeated in many battles, they shut themselves up with their leader in Ravenna and such other towns as were especially strong. 489 A.D. And the Goths laid siege to these places and captured them all, in one way or another, as it chanced in each case, except that they were unable to capture, either by surrender or by storm, the fortress of Caesena,[4] which is three hundred stades distant from Ravenna, and Ravenna itself, where Odoacer happened to be. For this city of Ravenna lies in a level plain at the extremity of the Ionian Gulf, lacking two stades of being on the sea, and it is so situated as not to be easily approached either by ships or by a land army. Ships cannot possibly put in to shore there because the sea itself prevents them by forming shoals for not less than thirty stades; consequently the beach at Ravenna, although to the eye of mariners it is very [9]near at hand, is in reality very far away by reason of the great extent of the shoal-water. And a land army cannot approach it at all; for the river Po, also called the Eridanus, which flows past Ravenna, coming from the boundaries of Celtica, and other navigable rivers together with some marshes, encircle it on all sides and so cause the city to be surrounded by water. In that place a very wonderful thing takes place every day. For early in the morning the sea forms a kind of river and comes up over the land for the distance of a day's journey for an unencumbered traveller and becomes navigable in the midst of the mainland, and then in the late afternoon it turns back again, causing the inlet to disappear, and gathers the stream to itself.[5] All those, therefore, who have to convey provisions into the city or carry them out from there for trade or for any other reason, place their cargoes in boats, and drawing them down to the place where the inlet is regularly formed, they await the inflow of the water. And when this comes, the boats are lifted little by little from the ground and float, and the sailors on them set to work and from that time on are seafaring men. And this is not the only place where this happens, but it is the regular occurrence along the whole coast in this region as far as the city of Aquileia. However, it does not always take place in the same way at every time, but when the light of the moon is faint, the advance of the sea is not strong either, but from the first[6] half-moon until the [11]second the inflow has a tendency to be greater. So much for this matter.

But when the third year had already been spent by the Goths and Theoderic in their siege of Ravenna, the Goths, who were weary of the siege, and the followers of Odoacer, who were hard pressed by the lack of provisions, came to an agreement with each other through the mediation of the priest of Ravenna, the understanding being that both Theoderic and Odoacer should reside in Ravenna on terms of complete equality. And for some time they observed the agreement; but afterward Theoderic caught Odoacer, as they say, plotting against him, and bidding him to a feast with treacherous intent slew him,[7] and in this way, after gaining the adherence of such of the hostile barbarians as chanced to survive, he himself secured the supremacy over both Goths and Italians. And though he did not claim the right to assume either the garb or the name of emperor of the Romans, but was called "rex" to the end of his life (for thus the barbarians are accustomed to call their leaders),[8] still, in governing his own subjects, he invested himself with all the qualities which appropriately belong to one who is by birth an emperor. For he was exceedingly careful to observe justice, he preserved the laws on a sure basis, he protected the land and kept it safe from the barbarians dwelling round about, and attained the highest possible degree of wisdom and manliness. And he himself committed scarcely a single act of injustice against his subjects, nor would he brook such conduct on the part of [13]anyone else who attempted it, except, indeed, that the Goths distributed among themselves the portion of the lands which Odoacer had given to his own partisans. And although in name Theoderic was a usurper, yet in fact he was as truly an emperor as any who have distinguished themselves in this office from the beginning; and love for him among both Goths and Italians grew to be great, and that too contrary to the ordinary habits of men. For in all states men's preferences are divergent, with the result that the government in power pleases for the moment only those with whom its acts find favour, but offends those whose judgment it violates. But Theoderic reigned for thirty-seven years, and when he died, he had not only made himself an object of terror to all his enemies, but he also left to his subjects a keen sense of bereavement at his loss. And he died in the following manner. 526 A.D.

Symmachus and his son-in-law Boetius were men of noble and ancient lineage, and both had been leading men[9] in the Roman senate and had been consuls. But because they practised philosophy and were mindful of justice in a manner surpassed by no other men, relieving the destitution of both citizens and strangers by generous gifts of money, they attained great fame and thus led men of the basest sort to envy them. Now such persons slandered them to Theoderic, and he, believing their slanders, put these two men to death, on the ground that they were setting about a revolution, and made their property confiscate to the public treasury. And a few days later, while he was dining, the servants set before him [15]the head of a great fish. This seemed to Theoderic to be the head of Symmachus newly slain. Indeed, with its teeth set in its lower lip and its eyes looking at him with a grim and insane stare, it did resemble exceedingly a person threatening him. And becoming greatly frightened at the extraordinary prodigy and shivering excessively, he retired running to his own chamber, and bidding them place many covers upon him, remained quiet. But afterwards he disclosed to his physician Elpidius all that had happened and wept for the wrong he had done Symmachus and Boetius. Then, having lamented and grieved exceedingly over the unfortunate occurrence, he died not long afterward. This was the first and last act of injustice which he committed toward his subjects, and the cause of it was that he had not made a thorough investigation, as he was accustomed to do, before passing judgment on the two men.

FOOTNOTES:

[1] Book III. ii. 7 ff., iv. 29 ff.

[2] Odoacer was defeated and shut up in Ravenna by Theoderic in 489, surrendered to him in 493, and was put to death in the same year. His independent rule (τυραννο) therefore lasted thirteen years.

[3] Meaning the whole Adriatic; cf. chap. xv. 16, note.

[4] Modern Cesena.

[5] He means that an estuary (πορθμός) is formed by the rising tide in the morning, and the water flows out again as the tide falls in the evening.

[6] From the first until the third quarter.

[7] See note in Bury's edition of Gibbon, Vol. IV. p. 180, for an interesting account of this event.

[8] This is a general observation; the title "rex" was current among the barbarians to indicate a position inferior to that of a βασιλεύς or "imperator"; cf. VI. xiv. 38.

[9] Probably a reminiscence of the "princeps senatus" of classical times.

II

526 A.D. After his death the kingdom was taken over by Atalaric, the son of Theoderic's daughter; he had reached the age of eight years and was being reared under the care of his mother Amalasuntha. For his father had already departed from among men. And not long afterward Justinian succeeded to the imperial power in Byzantium. 527 A.D. Now Amalasuntha, as guardian of her child, administered the government, and she proved to be endowed with wisdom and regard for justice in the highest degree, displaying to a great extent the masculine temper. As long as she stood at the head of the government she inflicted punish[17]ment upon no Roman in any case either by touching his person or by imposing a fine. Furthermore, she did not give way to the Goths in their mad desire to wrong them, but she even restored to the children of Symmachus and Boetius their fathers' estates. Now Amalasuntha wished to make her son resemble the Roman princes in his manner of life, and was already compelling him to attend the school of a teacher of letters. And she chose out three among the old men of the Goths whom she knew to be prudent and refined above all the others, and bade them live with Atalaric. But the Goths were by no means pleased with this. For because of their eagerness to wrong their subjects they wished to be ruled by him more after the barbarian fashion. On one occasion the mother, finding the boy doing some wrong in his chamber, chastised him; and he in tears went off thence to the men's apartments. And some Goths who met him made a great to-do about this, and reviling Amalasuntha insisted that she wished to put the boy out of the world as quickly as possible, in order that she might marry a second husband and with him rule over the Goths and Italians. And all the notable men among them gathered together, and coming before Amalasuntha made the charge that their king was not being educated correctly from their point of view nor to his own advantage. For letters, they said, are far removed from manliness, and the teaching of old men results for the most part in a cowardly and submissive spirit. Therefore the man who is to shew daring in

any work and be great in renown ought to be freed from the timidity which teachers inspire and to take his training in arms.[19] They added that even Theoderic would never allow any of the Goths to send their children to school; for he used to say to them all that, if the fear of the strap once came over them, they would never have the resolution to despise sword or spear. And they asked her to reflect that her father Theoderic before he died had become master of all this territory and had invested himself with a kingdom which was his by no sort of right, although he had not so much as heard of letters. "Therefore, O Queen," they said, "have done with these tutors now, and do you give to Atalaric some men of his own age to be his companions, who will pass through the period of youth with him and thus give him an impulse toward that excellence which is in keeping with the custom of barbarians."

When Amalasuntha heard this, although she did not approve, yet because she feared the plotting of these men, she made it appear that their words found favour with her, and granted everything the barbarians desired of her. And when the old men had left Atalaric, he was given the company of some boys who were to share his daily life,—lads who had not yet come of age but were only a little in advance of him in years; and these boys, as soon as he came of age, by enticing him to drunkenness and to intercourse with women, made him an exceptionally depraved youth, and of such stupid folly that he was disinclined to follow his mother's advice. Consequently he utterly refused to champion her cause, although the barbarians were by now openly leaguing together against her; for they were boldly commanding the [21]woman to withdraw from the palace. But Amalasuntha neither became frightened at the plotting of the Goths nor did she, womanlike, weakly give way, but still displaying the dignity befitting a queen, she chose out three men who were the most notable among the barbarians and at the same time the most responsible for the sedition against her, and bade them go to the limits of Italy, not together, however, but as far apart as possible from one another; but it was made to appear that they were being sent in order to guard the land against the enemy's attack. But nevertheless these men by the help of their friends and relations, who were all still in communication with them, even travelling a long journey for the purpose, continued to make ready the details of their plot against Amalasuntha.

And the woman, being unable to endure these things any longer, devised the following plan. Sending to Byzantium she enquired of the Emperor Justinian whether it was his wish that Amalasuntha, the daughter of Theoderic, should come to him; for she wished to depart from Italy as quickly as possible. And the emperor, being pleased by the suggestion, bade her come and sent orders that the finest of the houses in Epidamnus should be put in readiness, in order that when Amalasuntha should come there, she might lodge in it and after spending such time there as she wished might then betake herself to Byzantium. When Amalasuntha learned this, she chose out certain Goths who were energetic men and especially devoted [23]to her and sent them to kill the three whom I have just mentioned, as having been chiefly responsible for the sedition against her. And she herself placed all her possessions, including four hundred centenaria[10] of gold, in a single ship and embarked on it some of those most faithful to her and bade them sail to Epidamnus, and, upon arriving there, to anchor in its harbour, but to discharge from the ship nothing whatever of its cargo until she herself should send orders. And she did this in order that, if she should learn that the three men had been destroyed, she might remain there and summon the ship back, having no further fear from her enemies; but if it should chance that any one of them was left alive, no good hope being left her, she purposed to sail with all speed and find safety for herself and her possessions in the emperor's land. Such was the purpose with which Amalasuntha was sending the ship to Epidamnus; and when it arrived at the harbour of that city, those who had the money carried out her orders. But a little later, when the murders had been accomplished as she wished, Amalasuntha summoned the ship back and remaining at Ravenna strengthened her rule and made it as secure as might be.

FOOTNOTE:

[10] See Book I. xxii. 4; III. vi. 2 and note.

III

There was among the Goths one Theodatus by name, son of Amalafrida, the sister of Theoderic, a man already of mature years, versed in the Latin literature and the teachings of Plato, but without [25]any experience whatever in war and taking no part in active life, and yet extraordinarily devoted to the pursuit of money. This Theodatus had gained possession of most of the lands in Tuscany, and he was eager by violent methods to wrest the remainder from their owners. For to have a neighbour seemed to Theodatus a kind of misfortune. Now Amalasuntha was exerting herself to curb this desire of his, and consequently he was always vexed with her and resentful. He formed the plan, therefore, of handing over Tuscany to the Emperor Justinian, in order that, upon receiving from him a great sum of money and the senatorial dignity, he might pass the rest of his life in Byzantium. After Theodatus had formed this plan, there came from Byzantium to the chief priest of Rome two envoys, Hypatius, the priest of Ephesus, and Demetrius, from Philippi in Macedonia, to confer about a tenet of faith, which is a subject of disagreement and controversy among the Christians. As for the points in dispute, although I know them well, I shall by no means make mention of them; for I consider it a sort of insane folly to investigate the nature of God, enquiring of what sort it is. For man cannot, I think, apprehend even human affairs with accuracy, much less those things which pertain to the nature of God. As for me, therefore, I shall maintain a discreet silence concerning these matters, with the sole object that old and venerable beliefs may not be discredited. For I, for my part, will say nothing whatever about God save that He is altogether good and has all things in His power. But let each one say whatever he thinks he knows about these matters, both priest and layman.[27] As for Theodatus, he met these envoys secretly and directed them to report to the Emperor Justinian what he had planned, explaining what has just been set forth by me.

But at this juncture Atalaric, having plunged into a drunken revel which passed all bounds, was seized with a wasting disease.

Wherefore Amalasuntha was in great perplexity; for, on the one hand, she had no confidence in the loyalty of her son, now that he had gone so far in his depravity, and, on the other, she thought that if Atalaric also should be removed from among men, her life would not be safe thereafter, since she had given offence to the most notable of the Goths. For this reason she was desirous of handing over the power of the Goths and Italians to the Emperor Justinian, in order that she herself might be saved. And it happened that Alexander, a man of the senate, together with Demetrius and Hypatius, had come to Ravenna. For when the emperor had heard that Amalasuntha's boat was anchored in the harbour of Epidamnus, but that she herself was still tarrying, although much time had passed, he had sent Alexander to investigate and report to him the whole situation with regard to Amalasuntha; but it was given out that the emperor had sent Alexander as an envoy to her because he was greatly disturbed by the events at Lilybaeum which have been set forth by me in the preceding narrative,[11] and because ten Huns from the army in Libya had taken flight and reached Campania, and Uliaris, who was guarding Naples, had received them not at all against the will of Amalasuntha, and also because the Goths, in making war on the Gepaedes about[29] Sirmium,[12] had treated the city of Gratiana, situated at the extremity of Illyricum, as a hostile town. So by way of protesting to Amalasuntha with regard to these things, he wrote a letter and sent Alexander.

And when Alexander arrived in Rome, he left there the priests busied with the matters for which they had come, and he himself, journeying on to Ravenna and coming before Amalasuntha, reported the emperor's message secretly, and openly delivered the letter to her. And the purport of the writing was as follows: "The fortress of Lilybaeum, which is ours, you have taken by force and are now holding, and barbarians, slaves of mine who have run away, you have received and have not even yet decided to restore them to me, and besides all this you have treated outrageously my city of Gratiana, though it belongs to you in no way whatever. Wherefore it is time for you to consider what the end of these things will some day be." And when this letter had been delivered to her and she had read it, she replied in the following words: "One may reasonably expect an emperor who is great and lays claim to virtue to assist an orphan child who does not in the least comprehend what is being done, rather than for no cause at all to quarrel with him. For unless a struggle be waged on even terms, even the victory it gains brings no honour. But thou dost threaten Atalaric on account of Lilybaeum, and ten runaways, and a mistake, made by soldiers in going against their enemies, which through some misapprehension chanced to affect a friendly city. Nay! do not thus; do not thou thus, O Emperor, but call to mind [31]that when them wast making war upon the Vandals, we not only refrained from hindering thee, but quite zealously even gave thee free passage against the enemy and provided a market in which to buy the indispensable supplies,[13] furnishing especially the multitude of horses to which thy final mastery over the enemy was chiefly due. And yet it is not merely the man who offers an alliance of arms to his neighbours that would in justice be called their ally and friend, but also the man who actually is found assisting another in war in regard to his every need. And consider that at that time thy fleet had no other place at which to put in from the sea except Sicily, and that without the supplies bought there it could not go on to Libya. Therefore thou art indebted to us for the chief cause of thy victory; for the one who provides a solution for a difficult situation is justly entitled also to the credit for the results which flow from his help. And what could be sweeter for a man, O Emperor, than gaining the mastery over his enemies? And yet in our case the outcome is that we suffer no slight disadvantage, in that we do not, in accordance with the custom of war, enjoy our share of the spoils. And now thou art also claiming the right to despoil us of Lilybaeum in Sicily, which has belonged to the Goths from ancient times, a lone rock, O Emperor, worth not so much as a piece of silver, which, had it happened to belong to thy kingdom from ancient times, thou mightest in equity at least have granted to Atalaric as a reward for his services, since he lent thee assistance in the times of thy most pressing necessity." Such was the message which Amalasuntha wrote openly to the emperor; but [33]secretly she agreed to put the whole of Italy into his hands. And the envoys, returning to Byzantium, reported everything to the Emperor Justinian, Alexander telling him the course which had been decided upon by Amalasuntha, and Demetrius and Hypatius all that they had heard Theodatus say, adding that Theodatus enjoyed great power in Tuscany, where he had become owner of the most of the land and consequently would be able with no trouble at all to carry his agreement into effect. And the emperor, overjoyed at this situation, immediately sent to Italy Peter, an Illyrian by birth, but a citizen of Thessalonica, a man who was one of the trained speakers in Byzantium, a discreet and gentle person withal and fitted by nature to persuade men.

FOOTNOTES:

[11] Book IV. v. 11 ff.

[12] Near modern Mitrowitz.

[13] Cf. Book III. xiv. 5, 6.

IV

But while these things were going on as I have explained, Theodatus was denounced before Amalasuntha by many Tuscans, who stated that he had done violence to all the people of Tuscany and had without cause seized their estates, taking not only all private estates but especially those belonging to the royal household, which the Romans are accustomed to call "patrimonium." For this reason the woman called Theodatus to an investigation, and when, being confronted by his denouncers, he had been proved guilty without any question, she compelled him to pay back everything which he had wrongfully seized and then dismissed him. And since in this way she had given the greatest offence to the man, from that time she was on hostile terms with him, [35]exceedingly vexed as he was by reason of his fondness for money, because he was unable to continue his unlawful and violent practices.

> Oct. 10, 534 A.D.

At about this same time Atalaric, being quite wasted away by the disease, came to his end, having lived eight years in office. As for Amalasuntha, since it was fated that she should fare ill, she took no account of the nature of Theodatus and of what she had recently done to him, and supposed that she would suffer no unpleasant treatment at his hands if she should do the man some rather unusual favour. She accordingly summoned him, and when he came, set out to cajole him, saying that for some time she had known well that it was to be expected that her son would soon die; for she had heard the opinion of all the physicians, who agreed in their judgment, and had herself perceived that the body of Atalaric continued to waste away. And since she saw that both Goths and Italians had an unfavourable opinion regarding Theodatus, who had now come to represent the race of Theoderic, she had conceived the desire to clear him of this evil name, in order that it might not stand in his way if he were called to the throne. But at the same time, she explained, the question of justice disturbed her, at the thought that those who claimed to have been wronged by him already should find that they had no one to whom they might report what had befallen them, but that they now had their enemy as their master. For these reasons, then, although she invited him to the throne after his name should have been cleared in this way, yet it was necessary, she said, that he should be bound by the most solemn oaths that while the title of the office should [37]be conferred upon Theodatus, she herself should in fact hold the power no less than before. When Theodatus heard this, although he swore to all the conditions which Amalasuntha wished, he entered into the agreement with treacherous intent, remembering all that she had previously done to him. Thus Amalasuntha, being deceived by her own judgment and the oaths of Theodatus, established him in the office. And sending some Goths as envoys to Byzantium, she made this known to the Emperor Justinian.

But Theodatus, upon receiving the supreme power, began to act in all things contrary to the hopes she had entertained and to the promises he had made. And after winning the adherence of the relatives of the Goths who had been slain by her—and they were both numerous and men of very high standing among the Goths— he suddenly put to death some of the connections of Amalasuntha and imprisoned her, the envoys not having as yet reached Byzantium. Now there is a certain lake in Tuscany called Vulsina,[14] within which rises an island,[15] exceedingly small but having a strong fortress upon it. There Theodatus confined Amalasuntha and kept her under guard. Apr. 30, 535 A.D. But fearing that by this act he had given offence to the emperor, as actually proved to be the case, he sent some men of the Roman senate, Liberius and Opilio and certain others, directing them to excuse his conduct to the emperor with all their power by assuring him that Amalasuntha had met with no harsh treatment at his hands, although [39]she had perpetrated irreparable outrages upon him before. And he himself wrote in this sense to the emperor, and also compelled Amalasuntha, much against her will, to write the same thing.

Such was the course of these events. But Peter had already been despatched by the emperor on an embassy to Italy with instructions to meet Theodatus without the knowledge of any others, and after Theodatus had given pledges by an oath that none of their dealings should be divulged, he was then to make a secure settlement with him regarding Tuscany; and meeting Amalasuntha stealthily he was to make such an arrangement with her regarding the whole of Italy as would be to the profit of either party. But openly his mission was to negotiate with regard to Lilybaeum and the other matters which I have lately mentioned. For as yet the emperor had heard nothing about the death of Atalaric or the succession of Theodatus to the throne, or the fate which had befallen Amalasuntha. And Peter was already on his way when he met the envoys of Amalasuntha and learned, in the first place, that Theodatus had come to the throne; and a little later, upon reaching the city of Aulon,[16] which lies on the Ionian Gulf, he met there the company of Liberius and Opilio, and learned everything which had taken place, and reporting this to the emperor he remained there.

And when the Emperor Justinian heard these things, he formed the purpose of throwing the Goths and Theodatus into confusion; accordingly he wrote [41]a letter to Amalasuntha, stating that he was eager to give her every possible support, and at the same time he directed Peter by no means to conceal this message, but to make it known to Theodatus himself and to all the Goths. And when the envoys from Italy arrived in Byzantium, they all, with a single exception, reported the whole matter to the emperor, and especially Liberius; for he was a man unusually upright and honourable, and one who knew well how to shew regard for the truth; but Opilio alone declared with the greatest persistence that Theodatus had committed no offence against Amalasuntha. Now when Peter arrived in Italy, it so happened that Amalasuntha had been removed from among men. For the relatives of the Goths who had been slain by her came before Theodatus declaring that neither his life nor theirs was secure unless Amalasuntha should be put out of their way as quickly as possible. And as soon as he gave in to them, they went to the island and killed Amalasuntha,—an act which grieved exceedingly all the Italians and the Goths as well. For the woman had the strictest regard for every kind of virtue, as has been stated by me a little earlier.[17] Now Peter protested openly[18] to Theodatus and the other Goths that because this base deed had been committed by them, there would be war without truce between the emperor and themselves. But Theodatus, such was his stupid folly, while still holding the slayers of Amalasuntha in honour and favour kept trying to persuade Peter and the [43]emperor that this unholy deed had been committed by the Goths by no means with his approval, but decidedly against his will.

FOOTNOTES:

[14] Modern Bolsena.

[15] Marta; "now entirely uninhabited, but with a few steps cut in the rock which are said to have led to the prison of Amalasuntha."— HODGKIN.

[16] Modern Avlona in Albania.

[17] Chap. ii. 3.

[18] See Gibbon's note (chap. xli.), amplified in Bury's edition, Vol. IV. p. 304, for additional light on the part played by Justinian and Peter in this affair.

V

Meanwhile it happened that Belisarius had distinguished himself by the defeat of Gelimer and the Vandals. And the emperor, upon learning what had befallen Amalasuntha, immediately entered upon the war, being in the ninth year of his reign. And he first commanded Mundus, the general of Illyricum, to go to Dalmatia, which was subject to the Goths, and make trial of Salones.[19] Now Mundus was by birth a barbarian, but exceedingly loyal to the cause of the emperor and an able warrior. Then he sent Belisarius by sea with four thousand soldiers from the regular troops and the foederati,[20] and about three thousand of the Isaurians. And the commanders were men of note: Constantinus and Bessas from the land of Thrace, and Peranius from Iberia[21] which is hard by Media, a man who was by birth a member of the royal family of the Iberians, but had before this time come as a deserter to the Romans through enmity toward the Persians; and the levies of cavalry were commanded by Valentinus, Magnus, and Innocentius, and the infantry by Herodian, Paulus, Demetrius, and Ursicinus, while the leader of the Isaurians was Ennes. And there were also two hundred Huns as [45]allies and three hundred Moors. But the general in supreme command over all was Belisarius, and he had with him many notable men as spearmen and guards. And he was accompanied also by Photius, the son of his wife Antonina by a previous marriage; he was still a young man wearing his first beard, but possessed the greatest discretion and shewed a strength of character beyond his years. And the emperor instructed Belisarius to give out that his destination was Carthage, but as soon as they should arrive at Sicily, they were to disembark there as it obliged for some reason to do so, and make trial of the island. And if it should be possible to reduce it to subjection without any trouble, they were to take possession and not let it go again; but if they should meet with any obstacle, they were to sail with all speed to Libya, giving no one an opportunity to perceive what their intention was.

And he also sent a letter to the leaders of the Franks as follows: "The Goths, having seized by violence Italy, which was ours, have not only refused absolutely to give it back, but have committed further acts of injustice against us which are unendurable and pass beyond all bounds. For this reason we have been compelled to take the field against them, and it is proper that you should join with us in waging this war, which is rendered yours as well as ours not only by the orthodox faith, which rejects the opinion of the Arians, but also by the enmity we both feel toward the Goths." Such was the emperor's letter; and making a gift of money to them, he agreed to give more as soon as they should take an active part. And they with all zeal promised to fight in alliance with him.[47]

Now Mundus and the army under his command entered Dalmatia, and engaging with the Goths who encountered them there, defeated them in the battle and took possession of Salones. As for Belisarius, he put in at Sicily and took Catana. And making that place his base of operations, he took over Syracuse and the other cities by surrender without any trouble; except, indeed, that the Goths who were keeping guard in Panormus,[22] having confidence in the fortifications of the place, which was a strong one, were quite unwilling to yield to Belisarius and ordered him to lead his army away from there with all speed. But Belisarius, considering that it was impossible to capture the place from the landward side, ordered the fleet to sail into the harbour, which extended right up to the wall. For it was outside the circuit-wall and entirely without defenders. Now when the ships had anchored there, it was seen that the masts were higher than the parapet. Straightway, therefore, he filled all the small boats of the ships with bowmen and hoisted them to the tops of the masts. And when from these boats the enemy were shot at from above, they fell into such an irresistible fear that they immediately delivered Panormus to Belisarius by surrender. As a result of this the emperor held all Sicily subject and tributary to himself. And at that time it so happened that there fell to Belisarius a piece of good fortune beyond the power of words to describe. For, having received the dignity of the consulship because of his victory over the Vandals, while he was still holding this honour, and after he had won the whole of Sicily, on the last day of Dec. 31, 535 A.D.[49] his consulship, he marched into Syracuse, loudly applauded by the army and by the Sicilians and throwing golden coins to all. This coincidence, however, was not intentionally arranged by him, but it was a happy chance which befell the man, that after having recovered the whole of the island for the Romans he marched into Syracuse on that particular day; and so it was not in the senate house in Byzantium, as was customary, but there that he laid down the office of the consuls and so became an ex-consul. Thus, then, did good fortune attend Belisarius.

FOOTNOTES:

[19] Or Salona, near modern Spalato.

[20] Auxiliaries; see Book III. xi. 3, 4, and note.

[21] Corresponding roughly to modern Georgia, just south of the Caucasus.

[22] Modern Palermo.

VI

And when Peter learned of the conquest of Sicily, he was still more insistent in his efforts to frighten Theodatus and would not let him go. But he, turning coward and reduced to speechlessness no less than if he himself had become a captive with Gelimer,[23] entered into negotiations with Peter without the knowledge of any others, and between them they formed an agreement, providing that Theodatus should retire from all Sicily in favour of the Emperor Justinian, and should send him also a golden crown every year weighing three hundred litrae,[24] and Gothic warriors to the number of three thousand whenever he should wish; and that Theodatus himself should have no authority to kill any priest or senator, or to confiscate his property for the public treasury except by the decision of the emperor; and [51]that if Theodatus wished to advance any of his subjects to the patrician or some other senatorial rank this honour should not be bestowed by him, but he should ask the emperor to bestow it; and that the Roman populace, in acclaiming their sovereign, should always shout the name of the emperor first, and afterward that of Theodatus, both in the theatres and in the hippodromes and wherever else it should be necessary for such a thing to be done; furthermore, that no statue of bronze nor of any other material should ever be set up to Theodatus alone, but statues must always be made for both, and they must stand thus: on the right that of the emperor, and on the other side that of Theodatus. And after Theodatus had written in confirmation of this agreement he dismissed the ambassador.

But, a little later, terror laid hold upon the man's soul and brought him into fears which knew no bound and tortured his mind, filling him with dread at the name of war, and reminding him that if the agreement drawn up by Peter and himself did not please the emperor at all, war would straightway come upon him. Once more, therefore, he summoned Peter, who had already reached Albani,[25] for a secret conference, and enquired of the man whether he thought that the agreement would be pleasing to the emperor. And he replied that he supposed it would. "But if," said Theodatus, "these things do not please the man at all, what will happen then?" And Peter replied "After that you will have to wage war, most noble Sir." "But what is this," he said; "is it just, my dear ambassador?" And Peter, immediately taking him up, said "And how is it not just, my good Sir, that [53]the pursuits appropriate to each man's nature should be preserved?" "What, pray, may this mean?" asked Theodatus. "It means," was the reply, "that your great interest is to philosophize, while Justinian's is to be a worthy emperor of the Romans. And there is this difference, that for one who has practised philosophy it would never be seemly to bring about the death of men, especially in such great numbers, and it should be added that this view accords with the teachings of Plato, which you have evidently espoused, and hence it is unholy for you not to be free from all bloodshed; but for him it is not at all inappropriate to seek to acquire a land which has belonged from of old to the realm which is his own." Thereupon Theodatus, being convinced by this advice, agreed to retire from the kingship in favour of the Emperor Justinian, and both he and his wife took an oath to this effect. He then bound Peter by oaths that he would not divulge this agreement until he should see that the emperor would not accept the former convention. And he sent with him Rusticus, a priest who was especially devoted to him and a Roman citizen, to negotiate on the basis of this agreement. And he also entrusted a letter to these men.

So Peter and Rusticus, upon reaching Byzantium, reported the first decision to the emperor, just as Theodatus had directed them to do. But when the emperor was quite unwilling to accept the proposal, they revealed the plan which had been committed to writing afterwards. This was to the following effect:[55] "I am no stranger to royal courts, but it was my fortune to have been born in the house of my uncle while he was king and to have been reared in a manner worthy of my race; and yet I have had little experience of wars and of the turmoils which wars entail. For since from my earliest years I have been passionately addicted to scholarly disputations and have always devoted my time to this sort of thing, I have consequently been up to the present time very far removed from the confusion of battles. Therefore it is utterly absurd that I should aspire to the honours which royalty confers and thus lead a life fraught with danger, when it is possible for me to avoid them both. For neither one of these is a pleasure to me; the first, because it is liable to satiety, for it is a surfeit of all sweet things, and the second, because lack of familiarity with such a life throws one into confusion. But as for me, if estates should be provided me which yielded an annual income of no less than twelve centenaria,[26] I should regard the kingdom as of less account than them, and I shall hand over to thee forthwith the power of the Goths and Italians. For I should find more pleasure in being a farmer free from all cares than in passing my life amid a king's anxieties, attended as they are by danger after danger. Pray send a man as quickly as possible into whose hands I may fittingly deliver Italy and the affairs of the kingdom."

Such was the purport of the letter of Theodatus. And the emperor, being exceedingly pleased, replied as follows: "From of old have I heard by report that you were a man of discretion, but now, taught by experience, I know it by the decision you have reached [57]not to await the issue of the war. For certain men who in the past have followed such a course have been completely undone. And you will never repent having made us friends instead of enemies. But you will not only have this that you ask at our hands, but you will also have the distinction of being enrolled in the highest honours of the Romans. Now for the present I have sent Athanasius and Peter, so that each party may have surety by some agreement. And almost immediately Belisarius also will visit you to complete all the arrangements which have been agreed upon between us." After writing this the emperor sent Athanasius, the brother of Alexander, who had previously gone on an embassy to Atalaric, as has been said,[27] and for the second time Peter the orator, whom I have mentioned above,[28] enjoining upon them to assign to Theodatus the estates of the royal household, which they call "patrimonium"; and not until after they had drawn up a written document and had secured oaths to fortify the agreement were they to summon

Belisarius from Sicily, in order that he might take over the palace and all Italy and hold them under guard. And he wrote to Belisarius that as soon as they should summon him he should go thither with all speed.

FOOTNOTES:

[23] The captivity of Gelimer is described in Book IV. vii. 12-17; ix. 11-14.

[24] At present values "worth about £12,000."—HODGKIN.

[25] Modern Albano; on the Appian Way. Cf. Book VI. iv. 8.

[26] See Book I. xxii. 4; III. vi. 2, note.

[27] Chap. iii. 13.

[28] Chap. iii. 30, iv. 17 ff.

VII

But meantime, while the emperor was engaged in these negotiations and these envoys were travelling to Italy, the Goths, under command of Asinarius and Gripas and some others, had come with a great army into Dalmatia. And when they had reached the [59]neighbourhood of Salones, Mauricius, the son of Mundus, who was not marching out for battle but, with a few men, was on a scouting expedition, encountered them. A violent engagement ensued in which the Goths lost their foremost and noblest men, but the Romans almost their whole company, including their general Mauricius. And when Mundus heard of this, being overcome with grief at the misfortune and by this time dominated by a mighty fury, he went against the enemy without the least delay and regardless of order. The battle which took place was stubbornly contested, and the result was a Cadmean victory[29] for the Romans. For although the most of the enemy fell there and their rout had been decisive, Mundus, who went on killing and following up the enemy wherever he chanced to find them and was quite unable to restrain his mind because of the misfortune of his son, was wounded by some fugitive or other and fell. Thereupon the pursuit ended and the two armies separated. And at that time the Romans recalled the verse of the Sibyl, which had been pronounced in earlier times and seemed to them a portent. For the words of the saying were that when Africa should be held, the "world" would perish together with its offspring. This, however, was not the real meaning of the oracle, but after intimating that Libya would be once more subject to the Romans, it added this statement also, that when that time came Mundus would perish together with his son. For it runs as follows: "Africa capta Mundus cum nato peribit."[30] But since "mundus" in the Latin tongue has the force of "world," they thought [61]that the saying had reference to the world. So much, then, for this. As for Salones, it was not entered by anyone. For the Romans went back home, since they were left altogether without a commander, and the Goths, seeing that not one of their nobles was left them, fell into fear and took possession of the strongholds in the neighbourhood; for they had no confidence in the defences of Salones, and, besides, the Romans who lived there were not very well disposed towards them.

When Theodatus heard this, he took no account of the envoys who by now had come to him. For he was by nature much given to distrust, and he by no means kept his mind steadfast, but the present fortune always reduced him now to a state of terror which knew no measure, and this contrary to reason and the proper understanding of the situation, and again brought him to the opposite extreme of unspeakable boldness. And so at that time, when he heard of the death of Mundus and Mauricius, he was lifted up exceedingly and in a manner altogether unjustified by what had happened, and he saw fit to taunt the envoys when they at length appeared before him. And when Peter on one occasion remonstrated with him because he had transgressed his agreement with the emperor, Theodatus called both of them publicly and spoke as follows: "The position of envoys is a proud one and in general has come to be held in honour among all men; but envoys preserve for themselves these their prerogatives only so long as they guard the dignity of their embassy by the propriety of their own conduct. For men have sanctioned as just the killing of an envoy whenever he is either found to have insulted a [63]sovereign or has had knowledge of a woman who is the wife of another." Such were the words with which Theodatus inveighed against Peter, not because he had approached a woman, but, apparently, in order to make good his claim that there were charges which might lead to the death of an ambassador. But the envoys replied as follows: "The facts are not, O Ruler of the Goths, as thou hast stated them, nor canst thou, under cover of flimsy pretexts, wantonly perpetrate unholy deeds upon men who are envoys. For it is not possible for an ambassador, even if he wishes it, to become an adulterer, since it is not easy for him even to partake of water except by the will of those who guard him. And as for the proposals which he has received from the lips of him who has sent him and then delivers, he himself cannot reasonably incur the blame which arises from them, in case they be not good, but he who has given the command would justly bear this charge, while the sole responsibility of the ambassador is to have discharged his mission. We, therefore, shall say all that we were instructed by the emperor to say when we were sent, and do thou hear us quietly; for if thou art stirred to excitement, all thou canst do will be to wrong men who are ambassadors. It is time, therefore, for thee of thine own free will to perform all that thou didst promise the emperor. This, indeed, is the purpose for which we have come. And the letter which he wrote to thee thou hast already received, but as for the writing which he sent to the foremost of the Goths, to no others shall we give it than to them." When the leading men of the barbarians, who were present, heard this speech of the envoys, they bade [65]them give to Theodatus what had been written to them. And it ran as follows: "It has been the object of our care to receive you back into our state, whereat you may well be pleased. For you will come to us, not in order to be made of less consequence, but that you may be more honoured. And, besides, we are not bidding the Goths enter into strange or alien customs, but into those of a people with whom you were once familiar, though you have by chance been separated from them for a season. For these reasons Athanasius and Peter have been sent to you, and you ought to assist them in all things." Such was the purport of this letter. But after Theodatus had read everything, he not only decided not to perform in deed the promises he had made to the emperor, but also put the envoys under a strict guard.

But when the Emperor Justinian heard these things and what had taken place in Dalmatia, he sent Constantianus, who commanded the royal grooms, into Illyricum, bidding him gather an army from there and make an attempt on Salones, in whatever manner he might be able; and he commanded Belisarius to enter Italy with all speed and to treat the Goths as enemies. So Constantianus came to Epidamnus and spent some time there gathering an army. But in the meantime the Goths, under the leadership of Gripas, came with another army into Dalmatia and took possession of Salones; and Constantianus, when all his preparations were as complete as possible, departed from Epidamnus with his whole force and cast anchor at Epidaurus[31] which is on the right as [67]one sails into the Ionian

Gulf. Now it so happened that some men were there whom Gripas had sent out as spies. And when they took note of the ships and the army of Constantianus it seemed to them that both the sea and the whole land were full of soldiers, and returning to Gripas they declared that Constantianus was bringing against them an army of men numbering many tens of thousands. And he, being plunged into great fear, thought it inexpedient to meet their attack, and at the same time he was quite unwilling to be besieged by the emperor's army, since it so completely commanded the sea; but he was disturbed most of all by the fortifications of Salones (since the greater part of them had already fallen down), and by the exceedingly suspicious attitude on the part of the inhabitants of the place toward the Goths. And for this reason he departed thence with his whole army as quickly as possible and made camp in the plain which is between Salones and the city of Scardon.[32] And Constantianus, sailing with all his ships from Epidaurus, put in at Lysina,[33] which is an island in the gulf. Thence he sent forward some of his men, in order that they might make enquiry concerning the plans of Gripas and report them to him. Then, after learning from them the whole situation, he sailed straight for Salones with all speed. And when he had put in at a place close to the city, he disembarked his army on the mainland and himself remained quiet there; but he selected five hundred from the army, and setting over them as commander Siphilas, one of his own bodyguards, he commanded them to seize the narrow pass[34] which, as he had been informed, was in the [69]outskirts of the city. And this Siphilas did. And Constantianus and his whole land army entered Salones on the following day, and the fleet anchored close by. Then Constantianus proceeded to look after the fortifications of the city, building up in haste all such parts of them as had fallen down; and Gripas, with the Gothic army, on the seventh day after the Romans had taken possession of Salones, departed from there and betook themselves to Ravenna; and thus Constantianus gained possession of all Dalmatia and Liburnia, bringing over to his side all the Goths who were settled there. Such were the events in Dalmatia. And the winter drew to a close, and thus ended the first year of this war, the history of which Procopius has written.

FOOTNOTES:

[29] Proverbial for a victory in which the victor is slain; probably from the story of the Theban, or "Cadmean," heroes Eteocles and Polynices.

[30] See Bury's edition of Gibbon, Vol. IV. App. 15, for a discussion of this oracle.

[31] Modern Ragusa Vecchia.

[32] Near Sebenico.

[33] Modern Lesina.

[34] An important approach to the city from the west.

VIII

And Belisarius, leaving guards in Syracuse and Panormus, crossed with the rest of the army from Messana to Rhegium (where the myths of the poets say Scylla and Charybdis were), and every day the people of that region kept coming over to him. For since their towns had from of old been without walls, they had no means at all of guarding them, and because of their hostility toward the Goths they were, as was natural, greatly dissatisfied with their present government. And Ebrimous came over to Belisarius as a deserter from the Goths, together with all his followers; this man was the son-in-law of Theodatus, being married to Theodenanthe, his daughter. And [71]he was straightway sent to the emperor and received many gifts of honour and in particular attained the patrician dignity. And the army of Belisarius marched from Rhegium through Bruttium and Lucania, and the fleet of ships accompanied it, sailing close to the mainland. But when they reached Campania, they came upon a city on the sea, Naples by name, which was strong not only because of the nature of its site, but also because it contained a numerous garrison of Goths. And Belisarius commanded the ships to anchor in the harbour, which was beyond the range of missiles, while he himself made his camp near the city. He then first took possession by surrender of the fort which is in the suburb, and afterwards permitted the inhabitants of the city at their own request to send some of their notables into his camp, in order that they might tell what their wish was and, after receiving his reply, report to the populace. Straightway, therefore, the Neapolitans sent Stephanus. And he, upon coming before Belisarius, spoke as follows:

"You are not acting justly, O general, in taking the field against men who are Romans and have done no wrong, who inhabit but a small city and have over us a guard of barbarians as masters, so that it does not even lie in our power, if we desire to do so, to oppose them. But it so happens that even these guards had to leave their wives and children, and their most precious possessions in the hands of Theodatus before they came to keep guard over us. Therefore, if they treat with you at all, they will plainly be betraying, not the city, but themselves.[73] And if one must speak the truth with no concealment, you have not counselled to your advantage, either, in coming against us. For if you capture Rome, Naples will be subject to you without any further trouble, whereas if you are repulsed from there, it is probable that you will not be able to hold even this city securely. Consequently the time you spend on this siege will be spent to no purpose."

So spoke Stephanus. And Belisarius replied as follows:

"Whether we have acted wisely or foolishly in coming here is not a question which we propose to submit to the Neapolitans. But we desire that you first weigh carefully such matters as are appropriate to your deliberations and then act solely in accordance with your own interests. Receive into your city, therefore, the emperor's army, which has come to secure your freedom and that of the other Italians, and do not choose the course which will bring upon you the most grievous misfortunes. For those who, in order to rid themselves of slavery or any other shameful thing, go into war, such men, if they fare well in the struggle, have double good fortune, because along with their victory they have also acquired freedom from their troubles, and if defeated they gain some consolation for themselves, in that, they have not of their own free will chosen to follow the worse fortune. But as for those who have the opportunity to be free without fighting, but yet enter into a struggle in order to make their condition of slavery permanent, such men, even if it so happens that they conquer, have failed in the most vital point, and if in the battle they fare less happily than they wished, they will have, along with their general ill-[75]fortune, also the calamity of defeat. As for the Neapolitans, then, let these words suffice. But as for these Goths who are present, we give them the choice, either to array themselves hereafter on our side under the great emperor, or to go to their homes altogether immune from harm. Because, if both you and they, disregarding all these considerations, dare to raise arms against us, it will be necessary for us also, if God so wills, to treat whomever we meet as an enemy. If, however, it is the will of the Neapolitans to choose the cause of the emperor and thus to be rid of so cruel a slavery, I take it upon myself, giving you pledges, to promise that you will receive at our hands those benefits which the Sicilians lately hoped for, and with regard to which they were unable to say that we had sworn falsely."

Such was the message which Belisarius bade Stephanus take back to the people. But privately he promised him large rewards if he should inspire the Neapolitans with good-will toward the emperor. And Stephanus, upon coming into the city, reported the words of Belisarius and expressed his own opinion that it was inexpedient to fight against the emperor. And he was assisted in his efforts by Antiochus, a man of Syria, but long resident in Naples for the purpose of carrying on a shipping business, who had a great reputation there for wisdom and justice. But there were two men, Pastor and Asclepiodotus, trained speakers and very notable men among the Neapolitans, who were exceedingly friendly toward the Goths, and quite unwilling to have any change made in the present state of affairs. These two men, planning how they might block the negotiations, induced the multitude to demand many serious [77]concessions, and to try to force Belisarius to promise on oath that they should forthwith obtain what they asked for. And after writing down in a document such demands as nobody would have supposed that Belisarius would accept, they gave it to Stephanus. And he, returning to the emperor's army, shewed the writing to the general, and enquired of him whether he was willing to carry out all the proposals which the Neapolitans made and to take an oath concerning them. And Belisarius promised that they should all be fulfilled for them and so sent him back. Now when the Neapolitans heard this, they were in favour of accepting the general's assurances at once and began to urge that the emperor's army be received into the city with all speed. For he declared that nothing unpleasant would befall them, if the case of the Sicilians was sufficient evidence for anyone to judge by, since, as he pointed out, it had only recently been their lot, after they had exchanged their barbarian tyrants for the sovereignty of Justinian, to be, not only free men, but also immune from all difficulties. And swayed by great excitement they were about to go to the gates with the purpose of throwing them open. And though the Goths were not pleased with what they were doing, still, since they were unable to prevent it, they stood out of the way.

But Pastor and Asclepiodotus called together the people and all the Goths in one place, and spoke as follows: "It is not at all unnatural that the populace of a city should abandon themselves and their own safety, especially if, without consulting any of their notables, they make an independent decision regarding their all. But it is necessary for us, who are on [79]the very point of perishing together with you, to offer as a last contribution to the fatherland this advice. We see, then, fellow citizens, that you are intent upon betraying both yourselves and the city to Belisarius, who promises to confer many benefits upon you and to swear the most solemn oaths in confirmation of his promises. Now if he is able to promise you this also, that to him will come the victory in the war, no one could deny that the course you are taking is to your advantage. For it is great folly not to gratify every whim of him who is to become master. But if this outcome lies in uncertainty, and no man in the world is competent to guarantee the decision of fortune, consider what sort of misfortunes your haste is seeking to attain. For if the Goths overcome their adversaries in the war, they will punish you as enemies and as having done them the foulest wrong. For you are resorting to this act of treason, not under constraint of necessity, but out of deliberate cowardice. So that even to Belisarius, if he wins the victory over his enemies, we shall perhaps appear faithless and betrayers of our rulers, and having proved ourselves deserters, we shall in all probability have a guard set over us permanently by the emperor. For though he who has found a traitor is pleased at the moment of victory by the service rendered, yet afterwards, moved by suspicion based upon the traitor's past, he hates and fears his benefactor, since he himself has in his own possession the evidences of the other's faithlessness. If, however, we shew ourselves faithful to the Goths at the present time, manfully submitting to the danger, they will give us great rewards in case they win [81]the mastery over the enemy, and Belisarius, if it should so happen that he is the victor, will be prone to forgive. For loyalty which fails is punished by no man unless he be lacking in understanding. But what has happened to you that you are in terror of being besieged by the enemy, you who have no lack of provisions, have not been deprived by blockade of any of the necessities of life, and hence may sit at home, confident in the fortifications and in your garrison here?[35] And in our opinion even Belisarius would not have consented to this agreement with us if he had any hope of capturing the city by force. And yet if what he desired were that which is just and that which will be to our advantage, he ought not to be trying to frighten the Neapolitans or to establish his own power by means of an act of injustice on our part toward the Goths; but he should do battle with Theodatus and the Goths, so that without danger to us or treason on our part the city might come into the power of the victors."

When they had finished speaking, Pastor and Asclepiodotus brought forward the Jews, who promised that the city should be in want of none of the necessities, and the Goths on their part promised that they would guard the circuit-wall safely. And the Neapolitans, moved by these arguments, bade Belisarius depart thence with all speed. He, however, began the siege. And he made many attempts upon the circuit-wall, but was always repulsed, losing many of his soldiers, and especially those who laid some claim to valour. For the wall of Naples was inaccessible, on one side by reason of the sea, and on the other [83]because of some difficult country, and those who planned to attack it could gain entrance at no point, not only because of its general situation, but also because the ground sloped steeply. However, Belisarius cut the aqueduct which brought water into the city; but he did not in this way seriously disturb the Neapolitans, since there were wells inside the circuit-wall which sufficed for their needs and kept them from feeling too keenly the loss of the aqueduct.

FOOTNOTE:

[35] *i.e.* the Goths; cf. § 5 above.

IX

So the besieged, without the knowledge of the enemy, sent to Theodatus in Rome begging him to come to their help with all speed. But Theodatus was not making the least preparation for war, being by nature unmanly, as has been said before.[36] And they say that something else happened to him, which terrified him exceedingly and reduced him to still greater anxiety. I, for my part, do not credit this report, but even so it shall be told. Theodatus even before this time had been prone to make enquiries of those who professed to foretell the future, and on the present occasion he was at a loss what to do in the situation which confronted him—a state which more than anything else is accustomed to drive men to seek prophecies; so he enquired of one of the Hebrews, who had a great reputation for prophecy, what sort of an outcome the present war would have. The Hebrew commanded him to confine three groups of ten swine each in three huts, and after giving them respectively the names of Goths, Romans, and the soldiers of the [85]emperor, to wait quietly for a certain number of days. And Theodatus did as he was told. And when the appointed day had come, they both went into the huts and looked at the swine; and they found that of those which had been given the name of Goths all save two were dead, whereas all except a few were living of those which had received the name of the emperor's soldiers; and as for those which had been called Romans, it so happened that, although the hair of all of them had fallen out, yet about half of them survived. When Theodatus beheld this and divined the outcome of the war, a great fear, they say, came upon him, since he knew well that it would certainly be the fate of the Romans to die to half their number and be deprived of their possessions, but that the Goths would be defeated and their race reduced to a few, and that to the emperor would come, with the loss of but a few of his soldiers, the victory in the war. And for this reason, they say, Theodatus felt no impulse to enter into a struggle with Belisarius. As for this story, then, let each one express his views according to the belief or disbelief which he feels regarding it.

But Belisarius, as he besieged the Neapolitans both by land and by sea, was beginning to be vexed. For he was coming to think that they would never yield to him, and, furthermore, he could not hope that the city would be captured, since he was finding that the difficulty of its position was proving to be a very serious obstacle. And the loss of the time which was being spent there distressed him, for he was making his calculations so as to avoid being compelled to go against Theodatus and Rome in the winter season. Indeed he had already even given orders to the army to pack up, his intention [87]being to depart from there as quickly as possible. But while he was in the greatest perplexity, it came to pass that he met with the following good fortune. One of the Isaurians was seized with the desire to observe the construction of the aqueduct, and to discover in what manner it provided the supply of water to the city. So he entered it at a place far distant from the city, where Belisarius had broken it open, and proceeded to walk along it, finding no difficulty, since the water had stopped running because the aqueduct had been broken open. But when he reached a point near the circuit-wall, he came upon a large rock, not placed there by the hand of man, but a part of the natural formation of the place. And those who had built the aqueduct many years before, after they had attached the masonry to this rock, proceeded to make a tunnel from that point on, not sufficiently large, however, for a man to pass through, but large enough to furnish a passage for the water. And for this reason it came about that the channel of the aqueduct was not everywhere of the same breadth, but one was confronted by a narrow place at that rock, impassable for a man, especially if he wore armour or carried a shield. And when the Isaurian observed this, it seemed to him not impossible for the army to penetrate into the city, if they should make the tunnel at that point broader by a little. But since he himself was a humble person, and never had come into conversation with any of the commanders, he brought the matter before Paucaris, an Isaurian, who had distinguished himself among the guards of Belisarius. So Paucaris immediately reported the whole matter to the general. And Belisarius, being pleased by the report, took new courage, and by promising to reward [89]the man with great sums of money induced him to attempt the undertaking, and commanded him to associate with himself some of the Isaurians and cut out a passage in the rock as quickly as possible, taking care to allow no one to become aware of what they were doing. Paucaris then selected some Isaurians who were thoroughly suitable for the work, and secretly got inside the aqueduct with them. And coming to the place where the rock caused the passage to be narrow, they began their work, not cutting the rock with picks or mattocks, lest by their blows they should reveal to the enemy what they were doing, but scraping it very persistently with sharp instruments of iron. And in a short time the work was done, so that a man wearing a corselet and carrying a shield was able to go through at that point.

But when all his arrangements were at length in complete readiness, the thought occurred to Belisarius that if he should by act of war make his entry into Naples with the army, the result would be that lives would be lost and that all the other things would happen which usually attend the capture of a city by an enemy. And straightway summoning Stephanus, he spoke as follows: "Many times have I witnessed the capture of cities and I am well acquainted with what takes place at such a time. For they slay all the men of every age, and as for the women, though they beg to die, they are not granted the boon of death, but are carried off for outrage and are made to suffer treatment that is abominable and most pitiable. And the children, who are thus deprived of their proper maintenance and education, are forced to be slaves, and that, too, of the men who are the most odious of all—those on whose hands [91]they see the blood of their fathers. And this is not all, my dear Stephanus, for I make no mention of the conflagration which destroys all the property and blots out the beauty of the city. When I see, as in the mirror of the cities which have been captured in times past, this city of Naples falling victim to such a fate, I am moved to pity both it and you its inhabitants. For such means have now been perfected by me against the city that its capture is inevitable. But I pray that an ancient city, which has for ages been inhabited by both Christians and Romans, may not meet with such a fortune, especially at my hands as commander of Roman troops, not least because in my army are a multitude of barbarians, who have lost brothers or relatives before the wall of this town; for the fury of these men I should be unable to control, if they should capture the city by act of war. While, therefore, it is still within your power to choose and to put into effect that which will be to your advantage, adopt the better course and escape misfortune; for when it falls upon you, as it probably will, you will not justly blame fortune but your own judgment." With these words Belisarius dismissed Stephanus. And he went before the people of Naples weeping and reporting with bitter lamentations all that he had heard Belisarius say. But they, since it was not fated that the Neapolitans should become subjects of the emperor without chastisement, neither became afraid nor did they decide to yield to Belisarius.[93]

FOOTNOTE:

[36] Chap. iii. 1.

X

Then at length Belisarius, on his part, made his preparations to enter
the city as follows. Selecting at nightfall about four hundred men
and appointing as commander over them Magnus, who led a
detachment of cavalry, and Ennes, the leader of the Isaurians, he
commanded them all to put on their corselets, take in hand their
shields and swords, and remain quiet until he himself should give
the signal. And he summoned Bessas[37] and gave him orders to stay
with him, for he wished to consult with him concerning a certain
matter pertaining to the army. And when it was well on in the night,
he explained to Magnus and Ennes the task before them, pointed out
the place where he had previously broken open the aqueduct, and
ordered them to lead the four hundred men into the city, taking lights
with them And he sent with them two men skilled in the use of the
trumpet, so that as soon as they should get inside the circuit-wall,
they might be able both to throw the city into confusion and to notify
their own men what they were doing. And he himself was holding
in readiness a very great number of ladders which had been
constructed previously.

So these men entered the aqueduct and were proceeding toward the
city, while he with Bessas and Photius[38] remained at his post and
with their help was attending to all details. And he also sent to the
camp, commanding the men to remain awake and to keep their arms
in their hands. At the same time [95]he kept near him a large force—
men whom he considered most courageous. Now of the men who
were on their way to the city above half became terrified at the
danger and turned back. And since Magnus could not persuade them
to follow him, although he urged them again and again, he returned
with them to the general. And Belisarius, after reviling these men,
selected two hundred of the troops at hand, and ordered them to go
with Magnus. And Photius also, wishing to lead them, leaped into
the channel of the aqueduct, but Belisarius prevented him. Then
those who were fleeing from the danger, put to shame by the railings
of the general and of Photius, took heart to face it once more and

followed with the others. And Belisarius, fearing lest their operations should be perceived by some of the enemy, who were maintaining a guard on the tower which happened to be nearest to the aqueduct, went to that place and commanded Bessas to carry on a conversation in the Gothic tongue with the barbarians there, his purpose being to prevent any clanging of the weapons from being audible to them. And so Bessas shouted to them in a loud voice, urging the Goths to yield to Belisarius and promising that they should have many rewards. But they jeered at him, indulging in many insults directed at both Belisarius and the emperor. Belisarius and Bessas, then, were thus occupied.

Now the aqueduct of Naples is not only covered until it reaches the wall, but remains covered as it extends to a great distance inside the city, being carried on a high arch of baked brick. Consequently, when the men under the command of Magnus and Ennes had got inside the fortifications, they were [97]one and all unable even to conjecture where in the world they were. Furthermore, they could not leave the aqueduct at any point until the foremost of them came to a place where the aqueduct chanced to be without a roof and where stood a building which had entirely fallen into neglect. Inside this building a certain woman had her dwelling, living alone with utter poverty as her only companion; and an olive tree had grown out over the aqueduct. So when these men saw the sky and perceived that they were in the midst of the city, they began to plan how they might get out, but they had no means of leaving the aqueduct either with or without their arms. For the structure happened to be very high at that point and, besides, offered no means of climbing to the top. But as the soldiers were in a state of great perplexity and were beginning to crowd each other greatly as they collected there (for already, as the men in the rear kept coming up, a great throng was beginning to gather), the thought occurred to one of them to make trial of the ascent. He immediately therefore laid down his arms, and forcing his way up with hands and feet, reached the woman's house. And seeing her there, he threatened to kill her unless she should remain silent. And she was terror-stricken and remained speechless.

He then fastened to the trunk of the olive tree a strong strap, and threw the other end of it into the aqueduct. So the soldiers, laying hold of it one at a time, managed with difficulty to make the ascent. And after all had come up and a fourth part of the night still remained, they proceeded toward the wall; and they slew the garrison of two of the towers before the men in them [99]had an inkling of the trouble. These towers were on the northern portion of the circuit-wall, where Belisarius was stationed with Bessas and Photius, anxiously awaiting the progress of events. So while the trumpeters were summoning the army to the wall, Belisarius was placing the ladders against the fortifications and commanding the soldiers to mount them. But it so happened that not one of the ladders reached as far as the parapet. For since the workmen had not made them in sight of the wall, they had not been able to arrive at the proper measure. For this reason they bound two together, and it was only by using both of them for the ascent that the soldiers got above the level of the parapet. Such was the progress of these events where Belisarius was engaged.

But on the side of the circuit-wall which faces the sea, where the forces on guard were not barbarians, but Jews, the soldiers were unable either to use the ladders or to scale the wall. For the Jews had already given offence to their enemy by having opposed their efforts to capture the city without a fight, and for this reason they had no hope if they should fall into their hands; so they kept fighting stubbornly, although they could see that the city had already been captured, and held out beyond all expectation against the assaults of their opponents. But when day came and some of those who had mounted the wall marched against them, then at last they also, now that they were being shot at from behind, took to flight, and Naples was captured by storm. By this time the gates were thrown open and the whole Roman army came in. 536 A.D. But those who were stationed [101]about the gates which fronted the east, since, as it happened, they had no ladders at hand, set fire to these gates, which were altogether unguarded; for that part of the wall had been deserted, the guards having taken to flight. And then a great slaughter took place; for all of them were possessed with fury, especially those who had chanced to have a brother or other relative slain in the fighting at the wall. And they kept killing all whom they encountered, sparing neither old nor young, and dashing into the houses they made slaves of the women and children and secured the valuables as plunder; and in this the Massagetae outdid all the rest, for they did not even withhold their hand from the sanctuaries, but slew many of those who had taken refuge in them, until Belisarius, visiting every part of the city, put a stop to this, and calling all together, spoke as follows:

"Inasmuch as God has given us the victory and has permitted us to attain the greatest height of glory, by putting under our hand a city which has never been captured before, it behooves us on our part to shew ourselves not unworthy of His grace, but by our humane treatment of the vanquished, to make it plain that we have conquered these men justly. Do not, therefore, hate the Neapolitans with a boundless hatred, and do not allow your hostility toward them to continue beyond the limits of the war. For when men have been vanquished, their victors never hate them any longer. And by killing them you will not be ridding yourselves of enemies for the future, but you will be suffering a loss through the death of your subjects. Therefore, do these men no further harm, nor continue to give [103]way wholly to anger. For it is a disgrace to prevail over the enemy and then to shew yourselves vanquished by passion. So let all the possessions of these men suffice for you as the rewards of your valour, but let their wives, together with the children, be given back to the men. And let the conquered learn by experience what kind of friends they have forfeited by reason of foolish counsel."

After speaking thus, Belisarius released to the Neapolitans their women and children and the slaves, one and all, no insult having been experienced by them, and he reconciled the soldiers to the citizens. And thus it came to pass for the Neapolitans that on that day they both became captives and regained their liberty, and that they recovered the most precious of their possessions. For those of them who happened to have gold or anything else of value had previously concealed it by burying it in the earth, and in this way they succeeded in hiding from the enemy the fact that in getting back their houses they were recovering their money also. And the siege, which had lasted about twenty days, ended thus. As for the Goths who were captured in the city, not less than eight hundred in number, Belisarius put them under guard and kept them from all harm, holding them in no less honour than his own soldiers.

And Pastor, who had been leading the people upon a course of folly, as has been previously[39] set forth by me, upon seeing the city captured, fell into a fit of apoplexy and died suddenly, though he had neither been ill before nor suffered any harm from anyone. But Asclepiodotus, who was engaged in this [105]intrigue with him, came before Belisarius with those of the notables who survived. And Stephanus mocked and reviled him with these words: "See, O basest of all men, what evils you have brought to your fatherland, by selling the safety of the citizens for loyalty to the Goths. And furthermore, if things had gone well for the barbarians, you would have claimed the right to be yourself a hireling in their service and to bring to court on the charge of trying to betray the city to the Romans each one of us who have given the better counsel. But now that the emperor has captured the city, and we have been saved by the uprightness of this man, and you even so have had the hardihood recklessly to come into the presence of the general as if you had done no harm to the Neapolitans or to the emperor's army, you will meet with the punishment you deserve." Such were the words which Stephanus, who was deeply grieved by the misfortune of the city, hurled against Asclepiodotus. And Asclepiodotus replied to him as follows: "Quite unwittingly, noble Sir, you have been heaping praise upon us, when you reproach us for our loyalty to the Goths. For no one could ever be loyal to his masters when they are in danger, except it be by firm conviction. As for me, then, the victors will have in me as true a guardian of the state as they lately found in me an enemy, since he whom nature has endowed with the quality of fidelity does not change his conviction when he changes his fortune. But you, should their fortunes not continue to prosper as before, would readily listen to the overtures of their assailants. For he who has the disease of inconstancy of mind no sooner takes fright than he denies his pledge to those most dear."[107] Such were the words of Asclepiodotus. But the populace of the Neapolitans, when they saw him returning from Belisarius, gathered in a body and began to charge him with responsibility for all that had befallen them. And they did not leave him until they had killed him and torn his body into small pieces. After that they came to the house of Pastor, seeking for the man. And when the servants insisted that Pastor was dead, they were quite unwilling to believe them until they were shown the man's body. And the Neapolitans impaled him in the outskirts of the town. Then they begged Belisarius to pardon them for what they had done while moved with just anger, and receiving his forgiveness, they dispersed. Such was the fate of the Neapolitans.

FOOTNOTES:

[37] Cf. chap. v. 3.

[38] Cf. chap. v. 5.

[39] Chap. viii. 22.

XI

But the Goths who were at Rome and in the country round about had even before this regarded with great amazement the inactivity of Theodatus, because, though the enemy was in his neighbourhood, he was unwilling to engage them in battle, and they felt among themselves much suspicion toward him, believing that he was betraying the cause of the Goths to the Emperor Justinian of his own free will, and cared for nothing else than that he himself might live in quiet, possessed of as much money as possible. Accordingly, when they heard that Naples had been captured, they began immediately to make all these charges against him openly and gathered [109]at a place two hundred and eighty stades distant from Rome, which the Romans call Regata.[40] And it seemed best to them to make camp in that place; for there are extensive plains there which furnish pasture for horses. And a river also flows by the place, which the inhabitants call Decennovium[41] in the Latin tongue, because it flows past nineteen milestones, a distance which amounts to one hundred and thirteen stades, before it empties into the sea near the city of Taracina; and very near that place is Mt. Circaeum, where they say Odysseus met Circe, though the story seems to me untrustworthy, for Homer declares that the habitation of Circe was on an island. This, however, I am able to say, that this Mt. Circaeum, extending as it does far into the sea, resembles an island, so that both to those who sail close to it and to those who walk to the shore in the neighbourhood it has every appearance of being an island. And only when a man gets on it does he realize that he was deceived in his former opinion. And for this reason Homer perhaps called the place an island. But I shall return to the previous narrative.

The Goths, after gathering at Regata, chose as king over them and the Italians Vittigis, a man who, though not of a conspicuous house, had previously won great renown in the battles about Sirmium, when Theoderic was carrying on the war against the Gepaedes.[42] Theodatus, therefore, upon hearing this, rushed off in flight and took the road to Ra[111]venna. But Vittigis quickly sent Optaris, a Goth, instructing him to bring Theodatus alive or dead. Now it happened that this Optaris was hostile to Theodatus for the following cause. Optaris was wooing a certain young woman who was an heiress and also exceedingly beautiful to look upon. But Theodatus, being bribed to do so, took the woman he was wooing from him, and betrothed her to another. And so, since he was not only satisfying his own rage, but rendering a service to Vittigis as well, he pursued Theodatus with great eagerness and enthusiasm, stopping neither day nor night. And he overtook him while still on his way, laid him on his back on the ground, and slew him like a victim for sacrifice. Such was the end of Theodatus' life and of his rule, which had reached the third year.

Dec. 536 A.D.

And Vittigis, together with the Goths who were with him, marched to Rome. And when he learned what had befallen Theodatus, he was pleased and put Theodatus' son Theodegisclus under guard. But it seemed to him that the preparations of the Goths were by no means complete, and for this reason he thought it better first to go to Ravenna, and after making everything ready there in the best possible way, then at length to enter upon the war. He therefore called all the Goths together and spoke as follows:

"The success of the greatest enterprises, fellow-soldiers, generally depends, not upon hasty action at critical moments, but upon careful planning. For many a time a policy of delay adopted at the opportune moment has brought more benefit than the opposite course, and haste displayed at an unseason[113]able time has upset for many men their hope of success. For in most cases those who are unprepared, though they fight on equal terms so far as their forces are concerned, are more easily conquered than those who, with less strength, enter the struggle with the best possible preparation. Let us not, therefore, be so lifted up by the desire to win momentary honour as to do ourselves irreparable harm; for it is better to suffer shame for a short time and by so doing gain an undying glory, than to escape insult for the moment and thereby, as would probably be the case, be left in obscurity for all after time. And yet you doubtless know as well as I that the great body of the Goths and practically our whole equipment of arms is in Gaul and Venetia and the most distant lands. Furthermore, we are carrying on against the nations of the Franks a war which is no less important than this one, and it is great folly for us to proceed to another war without first settling that one satisfactorily. For it is natural that those who become exposed to attack on two sides and do not confine their attention to a single enemy should be worsted by their opponents. But I say that we must now go straight from here to Ravenna, and after bringing the war against the Franks to an end and settling all our other affairs as well as possible, then with the whole army of the Goths we must fight it out with Belisarius. And let no one of you, I say, try to dissemble regarding this withdrawal, nor hesitate to call it flight. For the title of coward, fittingly applied, has saved many, while the reputation for bravery which some men have gained at the [115]wrong time, has afterward led them to defeat. For it is not the names of things, but the advantage which comes from what is done, that is worth seeking after. For a man's worth is revealed by his deeds, not at their commencement, but at their end. And those do not flee before the enemy who, when they have increased their preparation, forthwith go against them, but those who are so anxious to save their own lives for ever that they deliberately stand aside. And regarding the capture of this city, let no fear come to any one of you. For if, on the one hand, the Romans are loyal to us, they will guard the city in security for the Goths, and they will not experience any hardship, for we shall return to them in a short time. And if, on the other hand, they harbour any suspicions toward us, they will harm us less by receiving the enemy into the city; for it is better to fight in the open against one's enemies. None the less I shall take care that nothing of this sort shall happen. For we shall leave behind many men and a most discreet leader, and they will be sufficient to guard Rome so effectively that not only will the situation here be favourable for us, but also that no harm may possibly come from this withdrawal of ours."

Thus spoke Vittigis. And all the Goths expressed approval and prepared for the journey. After this Vittigis exhorted at length Silverius, the priest[43] of the city, and the senate and people of the Romans, reminding them of the rule of Theoderic, and he urged upon all to be loyal to the nation of the Goths, binding them by the most solemn oaths to do so; and he chose out no fewer than four thousand men, [117]and set in command over them Leuderis, a man of mature years who enjoyed a great reputation for discretion, that they might guard Rome for the Goths. Then he set out for Ravenna with the rest of the army, keeping the most of the senators with him as hostages. And when he had reached that place, he made Matasuntha, the daughter of Amalasuntha, who was a maiden now of marriageable age, his wedded wife, much against her will, in order that he might make his rule more secure by marrying into the family of Theoderic. After this he began to gather all the Goths from every side and to organize and equip them, duly distributing arms and horses to each one; and only the Goths who were engaged in garrison duty in Gaul he was unable to summon, through fear of the Franks. These Franks were called "Germani" in ancient times. And the manner in which they first got a foothold in Gaul, and where they had lived before that, and how they became hostile to the Goths, I shall now proceed to relate.

FOOTNOTES:

[40] Near Terracina.

[41] The name is made from *decem* and *novem*, "nineteen,"— apparently a late formation. The "river" was in reality a canal, extending from Appii Forum to Terracina.

[42] Chap. iii. 15.

[43] Silverius was Pope 536-537 A.D.

XII

As one sails from the ocean into the Mediterranean at Gadira, the land on the left, as was stated in the preceding narrative,[44] is named Europe, while the land opposite to this is called Libya, and, farther on, Asia. Now as to the region beyond Libya[45] I am unable to speak with accuracy;[46] for it is almost wholly destitute of men, and for this reason the [119]first source of the Nile, which they say flows from that land toward Egypt, is quite unknown. But Europe at its very beginning is exceedingly like the Peloponnesus, and fronts the sea on either side. And the land which is first toward the ocean and the west is named Spain, extending as far as the alps of the Pyrenees range. For the men of this country are accustomed to call a narrow, shut-in pass "alps." And the land from there on as far as the boundaries of Liguria is called Gaul. And in that place other alps separate the Gauls and the Ligurians. Gaul, however, is much broader than Spain, and naturally so, because Europe, beginning with a narrow peninsula, gradually widens as one advances until it attains an extraordinary breadth. And this land is bounded by water on either side, being washed on the north by the ocean, and having on the south the sea called the Tuscan Sea. And in Gaul there flow numerous rivers, among which are the Rhone and the Rhine. But the course of these two being in opposite directions, the one empties into the Tuscan Sea, while the Rhine empties into the ocean. And there are many lakes[47] in that region, and this is where the Germans lived of old, a barbarous nation, not of much consequence in the beginning, who are now called Franks. Next to these lived the Arborychi,[48] who, together with all the rest of Gaul, and, indeed, Spain also, were subjects of the Romans from of old. And beyond them toward the east were settled the Thuringian bar[121]barians, Augustus, the first emperor, having given them this country.[49] And the Burgundians lived not far from them toward the south,[50] and the Suevi[51] also lived beyond the Thuringians, and the Alamani,[52] powerful nations. All these were settled there as independent peoples in earlier times.

But as time went on, the Visigoths forced their way into the Roman empire and seized all Spain and the portion of Gaul lying beyond[53] the Rhone River and made them subject and tributary to themselves. By that time it so happened that the Arborychi had become soldiers of the Romans. And the Germans, wishing to make this people subject to themselves, since their territory adjoined their own and they had changed the government under which they had lived from of old, began to plunder their land and, being eager to make war, marched against them with their whole people. But the Arborychi proved their valour and loyalty to the Romans and shewed themselves brave men in this war, and since the Germans were not able to overcome them by force, they wished to win them over and make the two peoples kin by intermarriage. This suggestion the Arborychi received not at all unwillingly; for both, as it happened, were Christians. And in this way they were united into one people, and came to have great power.

Now other Roman soldiers, also, had been stationed at the frontiers of Gaul to serve as guards. And these soldiers, having no means of returning to Rome, and at the same time being unwilling to yield [123]to their enemy[54] who were Arians, gave themselves, together with their military standards and the land which they had long been guarding for the Romans, to the Arborychi and Germans; and they handed down to their offspring all the customs of their fathers, which were thus preserved, and this people has held them in sufficient reverence to guard them even up to my time. For even at the present day they are clearly recognized as belonging to the legions to which they were assigned when they served in ancient times, and they always carry their own standards when they enter battle, and always follow the customs of their fathers. And they preserve the dress of the Romans in every particular, even as regards their shoes.

Now as long as the Roman polity remained unchanged,[55] the emperor held all Gaul as far as the Rhone River; but when Odoacer changed the government into a tyranny, 476 A.D. then, since the tyrant yielded to them, the Visigoths took possession of all Gaul as far as

the alps which mark the boundary between Gaul and Liguria. 493
A.D. But after the fall of Odoacer, the Thuringians and the Visigoths
began to fear the power of the Germans, which was now growing
greater (for their country had become exceedingly populous and
they were forcing into subjection without any concealment those
who from time to time came in their way), and so they were eager
to win the alliance of the Goths and Theoderic. And since Theoderic
wished to attach these peoples to himself, he did not refuse to
intermarry with them. Accordingly he betrothed to Alaric the
younger, who was then leader of the Visigoths, his [125]own
unmarried daughter Theodichusa, and to Hermenefridus, the ruler of
the Thuringians, Amalaberga, the daughter of his sister Amalafrida.
As a result of this the Franks refrained from violence against these
peoples through fear of Theoderic, but they began a war against the
Burgundians. But later on the Franks and the Goths entered into an
offensive alliance against the Burgundians, agreeing that each of the
two should send an army against them; and it was further agreed that
if either army should be absent when the other took the field against
the nation of the Burgundians and overthrew them and gained the
land which they had, then the victors should receive as a penalty
from those who had not joined in the expedition a fixed sum of gold,
and that only on these terms should the conquered land belong to
both peoples in common. So the Germans went against the
Burgundians with a great army according to the agreement between
themselves and the Goths; but Theoderic was still engaged with his
preparations, as he said, and purposely kept putting off the departure
of the army to the following day, and waiting for what would come
to pass. Finally, however, he sent the army, but commanded the
generals to march in a leisurely fashion, and if they should hear that
the Franks had been victorious, they were thenceforth to go quickly,
but if they should learn that any adversity had befallen them, they
were to proceed no farther, but remain where they were. So they
proceeded to carry out the commands of Theoderic, but meanwhile
the[127] Germans joined battle alone with the Burgundians. 534 A.D.
The battle was stubbornly contested and a great slaughter took place
on both sides, for the struggle was very evenly matched; but finally

the Franks routed their enemy and drove them to the borders of the land which they inhabited at that time, where they had many strongholds, while the Franks took possession of all the rest. And the Goths, upon hearing this, were quickly at hand. And when they were bitterly reproached by their allies, they blamed the difficulty of the country, and laying down the amount of the penalty, they divided the land with the victors according to the agreement made. And thus the foresight of Theoderic was revealed more clearly than ever, because, without losing a single one of his subjects, he had with a little gold acquired half of the land of his enemy. Thus it was that the Goths and Germans in the beginning got possession of a certain part of Gaul.

But later on, when the power of the Germans was growing greater, they began to think slightingly of Theoderic and the fear he inspired, and took the field against Alaric and the Visigoths. And when Alaric learned this, he summoned Theoderic as quickly as possible. And he set out to his assistance with a great army. In the meantime, the Visigoths, upon learning that the Germans were in camp near the city of Carcasiana,[56] went to meet them, and making a camp remained quiet. But since much time was being spent by them in blocking the enemy in this way, they began to be vexed, and seeing that their land [129]was being plundered by the enemy, they became indignant. And at length they began to heap many insults upon Alaric, reviling him on account of his fear of the enemy and taunting him with the delay of his father-in-law. For they declared that they by themselves were a match for the enemy in battle and that even though unaided they would easily overcome the Germans in the war. For this reason Alaric was compelled to do battle with the enemy before the Goths had as yet arrived. And the Germans, gaining the upper hand in this engagement, killed the most of the Visigoths and their ruler Alaric. 507 A.D. Then they took possession of the greater part of Gaul and held it; and they laid siege to Carcasiana with great enthusiasm, because they had learned that the royal treasure was there, which Alaric the elder in earlier times had taken as booty when he captured Rome.[57] Among these were also the treasures of

Solomon, the king of the Hebrews, a most noteworthy sight. 410 A.D. For the most of them were adorned with emeralds; and they had been taken from Jerusalem by the Romans in ancient times.[58] Then the survivors of the Visigoths declared Giselic, an illegitimate son of Alaric, ruler over them, Amalaric, the son of Theoderic's daughter, being still a very young child. And afterwards, when Theoderic had come with the army of the Goths, the Germans became afraid and broke up the siege. So they retired from there and took possession of the part of Gaul beyond the Rhone River as far as the [131]ocean. And Theoderic, being unable to drive them out from there, allowed them to hold this territory, but he himself recovered the rest of Gaul. Then, after Giselic had been put out of the way, he conferred the rule of the Visigoths upon his grandson Amalaric, for whom, since he was still a child, he himself acted as regent. And taking all the money which lay in the city of Carcasiana, he marched quickly back to Ravenna; furthermore, he continued to send commanders and armies into Gaul and Spain, thus holding the real power of the government himself, and by way of providing that he should hold it securely and permanently, he ordained that the rulers of those countries should bring tribute to him. And though he received this every year, in order not to give the appearance of being greedy for money he sent it as an annual gift to the army of the Goths and Visigoths. And as a result of this, the Goths and Visigoths, as time went on, ruled as they were by one man and holding the same land, betrothed their children to one another and thus joined the two races in kinship.

But afterwards, Theudis, a Goth, whom Theoderic had sent as commander of the army, took to wife a woman from Spain; she was not, however, of the race of the Visigoths, but belonged to the house of one of the wealthy inhabitants of that land, and not only possessed great wealth but also owned a large estate in Spain. From this estate he gathered about two thousand soldiers and surrounded himself with a force of bodyguards, and while in name he was a ruler over the Goths by the gift of Theoderic, he was in fact an out and out tyrant. And Theoderic, who was [133]wise and experienced in the highest degree, was afraid to carry on a war against his own slave, lest the Franks meanwhile should take the field against him, as they naturally would, or the Visigoths on their part should begin a revolution against him; accordingly he did not remove Theudis from his office, but even continued to command him, whenever the army went to war, to lead it forth. However, he directed the first men of the Goths to write to Theudis that he would be acting justly and in a manner worthy of his wisdom, if he should come to Ravenna and salute Theoderic. Theudis, however, although he carried out all the commands of Theoderic and never failed to send in the annual tribute, would not consent to go to Ravenna, nor would he promise those who had written to him that he would do so.

FOOTNOTES:

[44] Book III. i. 7.

[45] *i.e.* equatorial Africa.

[46] Cf. Book IV. xiii. 29.

[47] This vague statement is intended to describe the country west of the Rhine, at that time a land of forests and swamps.

[48] The people whom Procopius names Arborychi must be the Armorici. If so, they occupied the coast of what is now Belgium.

[49] Now south-eastern Germany.

[50] Now south-eastern France.

[51] Between the Germans and Burgundians.

[52] In modern Bavaria.

[53] *i.e.* west of the Rhone.

[54] *i.e.* the Visigoths.

[55] *i.e.* under a recognized imperial dynasty.

[56] In Gallia Narbonensis, modern Carcassone. Procopius has been misled. The battle here described was fought in the neighbourhood of Poitiers.

[57] Cf. Book III. ii. 14-24.

[58] At the capture of Jerusalem by Titus in 70 A.D. The treasures here mentioned were removed from Rome in 410 A.D. The remainder of the Jewish treasure formed part of the spoil of Gizeric, the Vandal. Cf. Book IV. ix. 5 and note.

XIII

After Theoderic had departed from the world, the Franks, now that there was no longer anyone to oppose them, took the field against the Thuringians, and not only killed their leader Hermenefridus but also reduced to subjection the entire people. But the wife of Hermenefridus took her children and secretly made her escape, coming to Theodatus, her brother, who was at that time ruling over the Goths. After this the Germans made an attack upon the Burgundians who had survived the former war,[59] and defeating them in battle confined their leader in one of the fortresses of the country and kept him under guard, while they reduced the people to subjection [135]and compelled them, as prisoners of war, to march with them from that time forth against their enemies, and the whole land which the Burgundians had previously inhabited they made subject and tributary to themselves. And Amalaric, who was ruling over the Visigoths, upon coming to man's estate, became thoroughly frightened at the power of the Germans and so took to wife the sister of Theudibert, ruler of the Germans, and divided Gaul with the Goths and his cousin Atalaric. The Goths, namely, received as their portion the land to the east of the Rhone River, while that to the west fell under the control of the Visigoths. And it was agreed that the tribute which Theoderic had imposed should no longer be paid to the Goths, and Atalaric honestly and justly restored to Amalaric all the money which he had taken from the city of Carcasiana. Then, since these two nations had united with one another by intermarriage, they allowed each man who had espoused a wife of the other people to choose whether he wished to follow his wife, or bring her among his own people. And there were many who led their wives to the people they preferred and many also who were led by their wives. But later on Amalaric, having given offence to his wife's brother, suffered a great calamity. For while his wife was of the orthodox faith, he himself followed the heresy of Arius, and he would not allow her to hold to her customary beliefs or to perform the rites of religion according to the tradition of her fathers, and, furthermore, because she was unwilling to conform to his customs, he held her in great dishonour. And since the woman was unable to bear this, she disclosed the whole matter to her brother. For this [137]reason, then, the Germans and Visigoths entered into war with each other. 531 A.D. And the battle which took place was for a long time very stoutly contested, but finally Amalaric was defeated, losing many of his men, and was himself slain. And Theudibert took his sister with all the money, and as much of Gaul as the Visigoths held as their portion. And the survivors of the vanquished emigrated from Gaul with their wives and children and went to Theudis in Spain, who was already acting the tyrant openly. Thus did the Goths and Germans gain possession of Gaul.

But at a later time[60] Theodatus, the ruler of the Goths, upon learning that Belisarius had come to Sicily, made a compact with the Germans, in which it was agreed that the Germans should have that portion of Gaul which fell to the Goths, and should receive twenty centenaria[61] of gold, and that in return they should assist the Goths in this war. But before he had as yet carried out the agreement he fulfilled his destiny. 526 A.D. It was for this reason, then, that many of the noblest of the Goths, with Marcias as their leader, were keeping guard in Gaul. It was these men whom Vittigis was unable to recall from Gaul,[62] and indeed he did not think them numerous enough even to oppose the Franks, who would, in all probability, overrun both Gaul and Italy, if he should march with his whole army against Rome. He therefore called together all who were loyal among the Goths and spoke as follows:

"The advice which I have wished to give you, [139]fellow-countrymen, in bringing you together here at the present time, is not pleasant, but it is necessary; and do you hear me kindly, and deliberate in a manner befitting the situation which is upon us. For when affairs do not go as men wish, it is inexpedient for them to go on with their present arrangements in disregard of necessity or fortune. Now in all other respects our preparations for war are in the best possible state. But the Franks are an obstacle to us; against them, our ancient enemies, we have indeed been spending both our lives and our money, but nevertheless we have succeeded in holding our own up to the present time, since no other hostile force has confronted us. But now that we are compelled to go against another foe, it will be necessary to put an end to the war against them, in the first place because, if they remain hostile to us, they will certainly array themselves with Belisarius against us; for those who have the same enemy are by the very nature of things induced to enter into friendship and alliance with each other. In the second place, even if we carry on the war separately against each army, we shall in the end be defeated by both of them. It is better, therefore, for us to accept a little loss and thus preserve the greatest part of our kingdom, than in our eagerness to hold everything to be destroyed by the enemy and lose at the same time the whole power of our supremacy. So my opinion is that if we give the Germans the provinces of Gaul which adjoin them, and together with this land all the money which Theodatus agreed to give them, they will not only be turned from their enmity against us, but will even lend us assistance in this war. But as to how at a later time, when matters [141]are going well for us, we may regain possession of Gaul, let no one of you consider this question. For an ancient saying[63] comes to my mind, which bids us 'settle well the affairs of the present.'"

Upon hearing this speech the notables of the Goths, considering the plan advantageous, wished it to be put into effect. Accordingly envoys were immediately sent to the nation of the Germans, in order to give them the lands of Gaul together with the gold, and to make an offensive and defensive alliance. Now at that time the rulers of the Franks were Ildibert, Theudibert, and Cloadarius, and they received Gaul and the money, and divided the land among them according to the territory ruled by each one, and they agreed to be exceedingly friendly to the Goths, and secretly to send them auxiliary troops, not Franks, however, but soldiers drawn from the nations subject to them. For they were unable to make an alliance with them openly against the Romans, because they had a little before agreed to assist the emperor in this war. So the envoys, having accomplished the mission on which they had been sent, returned to Ravenna. At that time also Vittigis summoned Marcias with his followers.

FOOTNOTES:

[59] Cf. chap. xii. 24 ff.

[60] Procopius resumes his narrative, which was interrupted by the digression beginning in chap. xii.

[61] Cf. Book I. xxii. 4; III. vi. 2 and note.

[62] Cf. chap. xi. 28.

[63] Cf. Thuc. i. 35, θέσθαι το ραρόν, "to deal with the actual situation"; Hor. *Od.* iii. 29, 32, "quod adest memento | Componere."

XIV

But while Vittigis was carrying on these negotiations, Belisarius was preparing to go to Rome. He accordingly selected three hundred men from the infantry forces with Herodian as their leader, and [143]assigned them the duty of guarding Naples. And he also sent to Cumae as large a garrison as he thought would be sufficient to guard the fortress there. For there was no stronghold in Campania except those at Cumae and at Naples. It is in this city of Cumae that the inhabitants point out the cave of the Sibyl, where they say her oracular shrine was; and Cumae is on the sea, one hundred and twenty-eight stades distant from Naples. Belisarius, then, was thus engaged in putting his army in order; but the inhabitants of Rome, fearing lest all the calamities should befall them which had befallen the Neapolitans, decided after considering the matter that it was better to receive the emperor's army into the city. And more than any other Silverius,[64] the chief priest of the city, urged them to adopt this course. So they sent Fidelius, a native of Milan, which is situated in Liguria, a man who had been previously an adviser of Atalaric (such an official is called "quaestor"[65] by the Romans), and invited Belisarius to come to Rome, promising to put the city into his hands without a battle. So Belisarius led his army from Naples by the Latin Way, leaving on the left the Appian Way, which Appius, the consul of the Romans, had made nine hundred years before[66] and to which he had given his name.

Now the Appian Way is in length a journey of five days for an unencumbered traveller; for it extends from Rome to Capua. And the breadth of this road is such that two waggons going in opposite directions [145]can pass one another, and it is one of the noteworthy sights of the world. For all the stone, which is mill-stone[67] and hard by nature, Appius quarried in another place[68] far away and brought there; for it is not found anywhere in this district. And after working these stones until they were smooth and flat, and cutting them to a polygonal shape, he fastened them together without putting concrete or anything else between them. And they were fastened together so securely and the joints were so firmly closed, that they give the appearance, when one looks at them, not of being fitted together, but of having grown together. And after the passage of so long a time, and after being traversed by many waggons and all kinds of animals every day, they have neither separated at all at the joints, nor has any one of the stones been worn out or reduced in thickness,—nay, they have not even lost any of their polish. Such, then, is the Appian Way.

But as for the Goths who were keeping guard in Rome, it was not until they learned that the enemy were very near and became aware of the decision of the Romans, that they began to be concerned for the city, and, being unable to meet the attacking army in battle, they were at a loss; but later, with the permission of the Romans, they all departed thence and proceeded to Ravenna, except that Leuderis, who commanded them, being ashamed, I suppose, because of the situation in which he found himself, remained there. And it so happened on that day that at the very same time when Belisarius and the emperor's [147]army were entering Rome through the gate which they call the Asinarian Gate, the Goths were withdrawing from the city through another gate which bears the name Flaminian; and Rome became subject to the Romans again after a space of sixty years, on the ninth day of the last month, which is called "December" by the Romans, in the eleventh year of the reign of the Emperor Justinian. 536 A.D. Now Belisarius sent Leuderis, the commander of the Goths, and the keys of the gates to the emperor, but he himself turned his attention to the circuit-wall, which had fallen into ruin in many places; and he constructed each merlon of the battlement with a wing, adding a sort of flanking wall on the left side,[69] in order that those fighting from the battlement against their assailants might never be hit by missiles thrown by those storming the wall on their left; and he also dug a moat about the wall of sufficient depth to form a very important part of the defences. And the Romans applauded the forethought of the general and especially the experience displayed in the matter of the battlement; but they marvelled greatly and were vexed that he should have thought it possible for him to enter Rome if he had any idea that he would be besieged, for it cannot possibly endure a siege because it cannot be supplied with provisions, since it is not on the sea, is enclosed by a wall of so huge a circumference,[70] and, above all, lying as it does in a very level plain, is naturally exceedingly [149]easy of access for its assailants. But although Belisarius heard all these criticisms, he nevertheless continued to make all his preparations for a siege, and the grain which he had in his ships when he came from Sicily he stored in public granaries and kept under guard, and he compelled all the Romans, indignant though they were, to bring all their provisions in from the country.

FOOTNOTES:

[64] Cf. chap. xi. 26, note.

[65] The quaestor held an important position as counsellor (πάρεδρος) of the emperor in legal matters. It was his function, also, to formulate and publish new laws.

[66] Built in 312 B.C. by the censor, Appius Claudius.

[67] Chiefly basalt. As built by Appius, however, the surface was of gravel; the stone blocks date from later years.

[68] Apparently an error, for lava quarries have been found along the road.

[69] i.e. on the left of the defender. The battlement, then, in horizontal section, had this form ⌐ ⌐ ⌐, instead of the usual series of straight merlons. Winged merlons were used on the walls of Pompeii; for an excellent illustration see Overbeck, *Pompeji*[4], p. 46.

[70] i.e. too great to be defended at every point: the total length of the circuit-wall was about twelve miles.

XV

At that time Pitzas, a Goth, coming from Samnium, also put himself and all the Goths who were living there with him into the hands of Belisarius, as well as the half of that part of Samnium which lies on the sea, as far as the river which flows through the middle of that district.[71] For the Goths who were settled on the other side of the river were neither willing to follow Pitzas nor to be subjects of the emperor. And Belisarius gave him a small number of soldiers to help him guard that territory. And before this the Calabrians and Apulians, since no Goths were present in their land, had willingly submitted themselves to Belisarius, both those on the coast and those who held the interior.

Among the interior towns is Beneventus,[72] which in ancient times the Romans had named "Maleventus," but now they call it Beneventus, avoiding the evil omen of the former name,[73] "ventus" having the meaning "wind" in the Latin tongue. For in[151] Dalmatia, which lies across from this city on the opposite mainland, a wind of great violence and exceedingly wild is wont to fall upon the country, and when this begins to blow, it is impossible to find a man there who continues to travel on the road, but all shut themselves up at home and wait. Such, indeed, is the force of the wind that it seizes a man on horseback together with his horse and carries him through the air, and then, after whirling him about in the air to a great distance, it throws him down wherever he may chance to be and kills him. And it so happens that Beneventus, being opposite to Dalmatia, as I have said, and situated on rather high ground, gets some of the disadvantage of this same wind. This city was built of old by Diomedes, the son of Tydeus, when after the capture of Troy he was repulsed from Argos. And he left to the city as a token the tusks of the Calydonian boar, which his uncle Meleager had received as a prize of the hunt, and they are there even up to my time, a noteworthy sight and well worth seeing, measuring not less than three spans around and having the form of a crescent. There, too, they say that Diomedes met Aeneas, the son of Anchises, when he was coming from Ilium, and in obedience to the oracle gave him the statue of Athena which he had seized as plunder in company with Odysseus, when the two went into Troy as spies before the city was captured by the Greeks. For they tell the story that when he fell sick at a later time, and made enquiry [153]concerning the disease, the oracle responded that he would never be freed from his malady unless he should give this statue to a man of Troy. And as to where in the world the statue itself is, the Romans say they do not know, but even up to my time they shew a copy of it chiselled on a certain stone in the temple of Fortune, where it lies before the bronze statue of Athena, which is set up under the open sky in the eastern part of the temple. And this copy on the stone represents a female figure in the pose of a warrior and extending her spear as if for combat; but in spite of this she has a chiton reaching to the feet. But the face does not resemble the Greek statues of Athena, but is altogether like the work of the ancient Aegyptians. The Byzantines, however, say that the Emperor Constantine dug up this statue in the forum which bears his name[74] and set it there. So much, then, for this.

In this way Belisarius won over the whole of that part of Italy which is south of the Ionian Gulf,[75] as far as Rome and Samnium, and the territory north of the gulf, as far as Liburnia, had been gained by Constantianus, as has been said.[76] But I shall now explain how Italy is divided among the inhabitants of the land. The Adriatic Sea[77] sends out a kind of outlet far into the continent and thus forms the Ionian Gulf, but it does not, as in other places where the sea enters the mainland, form an isthmus at its end.[155] For example, the so-called Crisaean Gulf, ending at Lechaeum, where the city of Corinth is, forms the isthmus of that city, about forty stades in breadth; and the gulf off the Hellespont, which they call the Black Gulf,[78] makes the isthmus at the Chersonese no broader than the Corinthian, but of about the same size. But from the city of Ravenna, where the Ionian Gulf ends, to the Tuscan Sea is not less than eight days' journey for an unencumbered traveller. And the reason is that the arm of the sea, as it advances,[79] always inclines very far to the right. And below this gulf the first town is Dryus,[80] which is now called Hydrus. And on the right of this are the Calabrians, Apulians, and Samnites, and next to them dwell the Piceni, whose territory extends as far as the city of Ravenna. And on the other side are the remainder of the Calabrians, the Bruttii, and the Lucani, beyond whom dwell the Campani as far as the city of Taracina, and their territory is adjoined by that of Rome. These peoples hold the shores of the two seas, and all the interior of that part of Italy. And this is the country called Magna Graecia in former times. For among the Bruttii are the Epizephyrian Locrians and the inhabitants of Croton and Thurii. But north of the gulf the first inhabitants are Greeks, called Epirotes, as far as the city of Epidamnus, which is situated on the sea. And adjoining this is the land of Precalis, beyond which [157]is the territory called Dalmatia, all of which is counted as part of the western empire. And beyond that point is Liburnia,[81] and Istria, and the land of the Veneti extending to the city of Ravenna. These countries are situated on the sea in that region. But above them are the Siscii and Suevi (not those who are subjects of the Franks, but another group), who inhabit the interior. And beyond these are settled the Carnii and Norici. On the right of these dwell the Dacians and Pannonians, who hold a number of towns, including Singidunum[82] and Sirmium, and extend as far as the Ister River. Now these peoples north of the Ionian Gulf were ruled by the Goths at the beginning of this war, but beyond the city of Ravenna on the left of the river Po the country was inhabited by the Ligurians.[83] And to the north of them live the Albani in an exceedingly good land called Langovilla, and beyond these are the nations subject to the Franks, while the country to the west is held by the Gauls and after them the Spaniards. On the right of the Po are Aemilia[84] and the Tuscan peoples, which extend as far as the boundaries of Rome. So much, then, for this.

FOOTNOTES:

[71] Probably either the Biferno or the Sangro.

[72] *sic* Procopius. The customary form "Beneventum" shews less clearly the derivation from "ventus" which Procopius favours. Other possible explanations are "bene" + "venio" or "bene" + (suff.) "entum."

[73] Cf. Pliny III. xi. 16, § 105, who says that the name was originally "Maleventum," on account of its unwholesome air.

[74] The Forum of Constantine was a short distance west of the Hippodrome. One of its principle monuments, a huge porphyry column, still stands and is known as the "Burnt Column."

[75] *i.e.* the Adriatic Sea; see note 4.

[76] Chap. vii. 36.

[77] By the "Adriatic" is meant the part of the Mediterranean which lies between Africa on the south, Sicily and Italy on the west, and Greece and Epirus on the east; Procopius' "Ionian Gulf" is therefore our Adriatic Sea.

[78] Now the Gulf of Saros, north and west of the Gallipoli peninsula.

[79] *i.e.* to the north-west. Procopius means that the Adriatic should incline at its upper end more toward the left (the west) in order to form the isthmus which he is surprised to find lacking.

[80] Hydruntum; cf. Book III. i. 9, note.

[81] Modern Croatia.

[82] Modern Belgrade.

[83] Procopius seems to have erred: Liguria, as well as Aemilia (below), was south of the Po. Cf. chap. xii. 4, where Liguria is represented as extending to the Alps.

[84] Whose capital was Placentia (Piacenzo).

XVI

So Belisarius took possession of all the territory of Rome as far as the river Tiber, and strengthened it. And when all had been settled by him in the best [159]possible manner, he gave to Constantinus a large number of his own guards together with many spearmen, including the Massagetae Zarter, Chorsomanus, and Aeschmanus, and an army besides, commanding him to go into Tuscany, in order to win over the towns of that region. And he gave orders to Bessas to take possession of Narnia, a very strong city in Tuscany. Now this Bessas was a Goth by birth, one of those who had dwelt in Thrace from of old and had not followed Theoderic when he led the Gothic nation thence into Italy, and he was an energetic man and a capable warrior. For he was both a general of the first rank, and a skilful man in action. And Bessas took Narnia not at all against the will of the inhabitants, and Constantinus won over Spolitium[85] and Perusia[86] and certain other towns without any trouble. For the Tuscans received him into their cities willingly. So after establishing a garrison in Spolitium, he himself remained quietly with his army in Perusia, the first city in Tuscany.

Now when Vittigis heard this, he sent against them an army with Unilas and Pissas as its commanders. And Constantinus confronted these troops in the outskirts of Perusia and engaged with them. The battle was at first evenly disputed, since the barbarians were superior in numbers, but afterwards the Romans by their valour gained the upper hand and routed the enemy, and while they were fleeing in complete disorder the Romans killed almost all of them; and they captured alive the commanders of the enemy and sent them to Belisarius. Now when Vittigis heard this, he was no longer [161]willing to remain quietly in Ravenna, where he was embarrassed by the absence of Marcias and his men, who had not yet come from Gaul. So he sent to Dalmatia a great army with Asinarius and Uligisalus as its commanders, in order to recover Dalmatia for the Gothic rule. And he directed them to add to their own troops an army from the land of the Suevi, composed of the barbarians there, and then to proceed directly to Dalmatia and Salones. And he also sent with them many ships of war, in order that they might be able to besiege Salones both by land and by sea. But he himself was hastening to go with his whole army against Belisarius and Rome, leading against him horsemen and infantry to the number of not less than one hundred and fifty thousand, and the most of them as well as their horses were clad in armour.

So Asinarius, upon reaching the country of the Suevi, began to gather the army of the barbarians, while Uligisalus alone led the Goths into Liburnia. And when the Romans engaged with them at a place called Scardon, they were defeated in the battle and retired to the city of Burnus; and there Uligisalus awaited his colleague. But Constantianus, upon hearing of the preparations of Asinarius, became afraid for Salones, and summoned the soldiers who were holding all the fortresses in that region. He then dug a moat around the whole circuit-wall and made all the other preparations for the siege in the best manner possible. And Asinarius, after gathering an exceedingly large army of barbarians, came to the [163]city of Burnus. There he joined Uligisalus and the Gothic army and proceeded to Salones. And they made a stockade about the circuit-wall, and also, filling their ships with soldiers, kept guard over the side of the fortifications which faced the sea. In this manner they proceeded to besiege Salones both by land and by sea; but the Romans suddenly made an attack upon the ships of the enemy and turned them to flight, and many of them they sunk, men and all, and also captured many without their crews. However, the Goths did not raise the siege, but maintained it vigorously and kept the Romans still more closely confined to the city than before. Such, then, were the fortunes of the Roman and Gothic armies in Dalmatia.

But Vittigis, upon hearing from the natives who came from Rome that the army which Belisarius had was very small, began to repent of his withdrawal from Rome, and was no longer able to endure the situation, but was now so carried away by fury that he advanced against them. And on his way thither he fell in with a priest who was coming from Rome. Whereupon they say that Vittigis in great excitement enquired of this man whether Belisarius was still in Rome, shewing that he was afraid he would not be able to catch him, but that Belisarius would forestall him by running away. But the priest, they say, replied that he need not be at all concerned about that; for he, the priest, was able to guarantee that Belisarius would never resort to flight, but was remaining where he was. But Vittigis, they say, [165]kept hastening still more than before, praying that he might see with his own eyes the walls of Rome before Belisarius made his escape from the city.

FOOTNOTES:

[85] Modern Spoleto.

[86] Modern Perugia.

XVII

But Belisarius, when he heard that the Goths were marching against him with their whole force, was in a dilemma. For he was unwilling, on the one hand, to dispense with the troops of Constantinus and Bessas, especially since his army was exceedingly small, and, on the other, it seemed to him inexpedient to abandon the strongholds in Tuscany, lest the Goths should hold these as fortresses against the Romans. So after considering the matter he sent word to Constantinus and Bessas to leave garrisons in the positions which absolutely required them, large enough to guard them, while they themselves with the rest of the army should come to Rome with all speed. And Constantinus acted accordingly. For he established garrisons in Perusia and Spolitium, and with all the rest of his troops marched off to Rome. But while Bessas, in a more leisurely manner, was making his dispositions in Narnia, it so happened that, since the enemy were passing that way, the plains in the outskirts of the city were filled with Goths. These were an advance guard preceding the rest of the army; and Bessas engaged with them and unexpectedly routed those whom he encountered and killed many; but then, since he was overpowered by their superior numbers, he retired into Narnia. And [167]leaving a garrison there according to the instructions of Belisarius, he went with all speed to Rome, and reported that the enemy would be at hand almost instantly. For Narnia is only three hundred and fifty stades distant from Rome. But Vittigis made no attempt at all to capture Perusia and Spolitium; for these places are exceedingly strong and he was quite unwilling that his time should be wasted there, his one desire having come to be to find Belisarius not yet fled from Rome. Moreover, even when he learned that Narnia also was held by the enemy, he was unwilling to attempt anything there, knowing that the place was difficult of access and on steep ground besides; for it is situated on a lofty hill. And the river Narnus flows by the foot of the hill, and it is this which has given the city its name. There are two roads leading up to the city, the one on the east, and the other on the west. One of these is very narrow and difficult by reason of precipitous rocks, while the other cannot be reached except by way of the bridge which spans the river and provides a passage over it at that point. This bridge was built by Caesar Augustus in early times, and is a very noteworthy sight; for its arches are the highest of any known to us.

So Vittigis, not enduring to have his time wasted there, departed thence with all speed and went with the whole army against Rome, making the journey [169]through Sabine territory. Feb. 21, 537 A.D.And when he drew near to Rome, and was not more than fourteen stades away from it, he came upon a bridge over the Tiber River.[87] There a little while before Belisarius had built a tower, furnished it with gates, and stationed in it a guard of soldiers, not because this is the only point at which the Tiber could be crossed by the enemy (for there are both boats and bridges at many places along the river), but because he wished the enemy to have to spend more time in the journey, since he was expecting another army from the emperor, and also in order that the Romans might bring in still more provisions. For if the barbarians, repulsed at that point, should try to cross on a bridge somewhere else, he thought that not less than twenty days would be consumed by them, and if they wished to launch boats in the Tiber to the necessary number, a still longer time would probably be wasted by them. These, then, were the considerations which led him to establish the garrison at that point; and the Goths bivouacked there that day, being at a loss and supposing that they would be obliged to storm the tower on the following day; but twenty-two deserters came to them, men who were barbarians by race but Roman soldiers, from the cavalry troop commanded by Innocentius.[88] Just at that time it occurred to Belisarius to establish a camp near the Tiber River, in order that they might hinder still more the crossing of the enemy and make some kind of a display of their own daring [171]to their opponents. But all the soldiers who, as has been stated, were keeping guard at the bridge, being overcome with terror at the throng of Goths and quailing at the magnitude of their danger, abandoned by night the tower they were guarding and rushed off in flight. But thinking that they could not enter Rome, they stealthily marched off toward

Campania, either because they were afraid of the punishment the general would inflict or because they were ashamed to appear before their comrades.

FOOTNOTES:

[87] The Mulvian Bridge.

[88] Cf. chap. v. 3.

XVIII

On the following day the Goths destroyed the gates of the tower with no trouble and made the crossing, since no one tried to oppose them. But Belisarius, who had not as yet learned what had happened to the garrison, was bringing up a thousand horsemen to the bridge over the river, in order to look over the ground and decide where it would be best for his forces to make camp. But when they had come rather close, they met the enemy already across the river, and not at all willingly they engaged with some of them. And the battle was carried on by horsemen on both sides. Then Belisarius, though he was safe before, would no longer keep the general's post, but began to fight in the front ranks like a soldier; and consequently the cause of the Romans was thrown into great danger, for the whole decision of the war rested with him. But it happened that the horse he was riding at that time was unusually experienced in warfare and knew well [173]how to save his rider; and his whole body was dark grey, except that his face from the top of his head to the nostrils was the purest white. Such a horse the Greeks call "phalius"[89] and the barbarians "balan." And it so happened that the most of the Goths threw their javelins and other missiles at him and at Belisarius for the following reason. Those deserters who on the previous day had come to the Goths, when they saw Belisarius fighting in the front ranks, knowing well that, if he should fall, the cause of the Romans would be ruined instantly, cried aloud urging them to "shoot at the white-faced horse." Consequently this saying was passed around and reached the whole Gothic army, and they did not question it at all, since they were in a great tumult of fighting, nor did they know clearly that it referred to Belisarius. But conjecturing that it was not by mere accident that the saying had gained such currency as to reach all, the most of them, neglecting all others, began to shoot at Belisarius. And every man among them who laid any claim to valour was immediately possessed with a great eagerness to win honour, and getting as close as possible they kept trying to lay hold of him and in a great fury kept striking with their spears and swords. But Belisarius himself, turning from side to side, kept killing as they came those who encountered him, and he also profited very greatly by the loyalty of his own spearmen and guards in this moment of danger. For they all surrounded [175]him and made a display of valour such, I imagine, as has never been shewn by any man in the world to this day; for, holding out their shields in defence of both the general and his horse, they not only received all the missiles, but also forced back and beat off those who from time to time assailed him. And thus the whole engagement was centred about the body of one man. In this struggle there fell among the Goths no fewer than a thousand, and they were men who fought in the front ranks; and of the household of Belisarius many of the noblest were slain, and Maxentius, the spearman, after making a display of great exploits against the enemy. But by some chance Belisarius was neither wounded nor hit by a missile on that day, although the battle was waged around him alone.

Finally by their valour the Romans turned the enemy to flight, and an exceedingly great multitude of barbarians fled until they reached their main army. For there the Gothic infantry, being entirely fresh, withstood their enemy and forced them back without any trouble. And when another body of cavalry in turn reinforced the Goths, the Romans fled at top speed until they reached a certain hill, which they climbed, and there held their position. But the enemy's horsemen were upon them directly, and a second cavalry battle took place. There Valentinus, the groom of Photius, the son of Antonina, made a remarkable exhibition of valour. For by leaping alone into the throng of the enemy he opposed himself to the onrush of the Goths and thus saved his companions. In this way the Romans escaped, and arrived at the fortifications of Rome, and the barbarians in pursuit pressed upon them [177]as far as the wall by the gate which has been named the Salarian Gate.[90] But the people of Rome, fearing lest the enemy should rush in together with the fugitives and thus get inside the fortifications, were quite unwilling to open the gates, although Belisarius urged them again and again and called upon them with threats to do so. For, on the one hand, those who peered out of the tower were unable to recognise the man, for his face and his whole head were covered with gore and dust, and at the same time no one was able to see very clearly, either; for it was late in the day, about sunset. Moreover, the Romans had no reason to suppose that the general survived; for those who had come in flight from the rout which had taken place earlier reported that Belisarius had died fighting bravely in the front ranks. So the throng of the enemy, which had rushed up in strength and possessed with great fury, were purposing to cross the moat straightway and attack the fugitives there; and the Romans, finding themselves massed along the wall, after they had come inside the moat, and so close together that they touched one another, were being crowded into a small space. Those inside the fortifications, however, since they were without a general and altogether unprepared, and being in a panic of fear for themselves and for the city, were quite unable to defend their own men, although these were now in so perilous a situation.

Then a daring thought came to Belisarius, which unexpectedly saved the day for the Romans. For urging on all his men he suddenly fell upon the [179]enemy. And they, even before this, had been in great disorder because of the darkness and the fact that they were making a pursuit, and now when, much to their surprise, they saw the fugitives attacking them, they supposed that another army also had come to their assistance from the city, and so were thrown into a great panic and all fled immediately at top speed. But Belisarius by no means rushed out to pursue them, but returned straightway to the wall. And at this the Romans took courage and received him and all his men into the city. So narrowly did Belisarius and the emperor's cause escape peril; and the battle which had begun early in the morning did not end until night. And those who distinguished themselves above all others by their valour in this battle were, among the Romans, Belisarius, and among the Goths, Visandus Vandalarius, who had fallen upon Belisarius at the first when the battle took place about him, and did not desist until he had received thirteen wounds on his body and fell. And since he was supposed to have died immediately, he was not cared for by his companions, although they were victorious, and he lay there with the dead. But on the third day, when the barbarians had made camp hard by the circuit-wall of Rome and had sent some men in order to bury their dead and to perform the customary rites of burial, those who were searching out the bodies of the fallen found Visandus Vandalarius with life still in him, and one of his companions entreated him to speak some word to him. But he could not do even this, for the inside of his body was on fire because of the lack of food and the thirst caused by his suffering, and so he nodded to him to put water into his [181]mouth. Then when he had drunk and become himself again, they lifted and carried him to the camp. And Visandus Vandalarius won a great name for this deed among the Goths, and he lived on a very considerable time, enjoying the greatest renown. This, then, took place on the third day after the battle.

But at that time Belisarius, after reaching safety with his followers, gathered the soldiers and almost the whole Roman populace to the wall, and commanded them to burn many fires and keep watch throughout the whole night. And going about the circuit of the fortifications, he set everything in order and put one of his commanders in charge of each gate. But Bessas, who took command of the guard at the gate called the Praenestine,[91] sent a messenger to Belisarius with orders to say that the city was held by the enemy, who had broken in through another gate which is across the Tiber River[92] and bears the name of Pancratius, a holy man. And all those who were in the company of Belisarius, upon hearing this, urged him to save himself as quickly as possible through some other gate. He, however, neither became panic-stricken, nor did he hesitate to declare that the report was false. And he also sent some of his horsemen across the Tiber with all speed, and they, after looking over the ground there, brought back word that no hostile attack had been made on the city in that quarter. He therefore sent immediately to each gate and instructed the commanders everywhere that, whenever they heard that the enemy had broken in at any other part of [183]the fortifications, they should not try to assist in the defence nor abandon their post, but should remain quiet; for he himself would take care of such matters. And he did this in order that they might not be thrown into disorder a second time by a rumour which was not true.

But Vittigis, while the Romans were still in great confusion, sent to the Salarian Gate[93] one of his commanders, Vacis by name, a man of no mean station. And when he had arrived there, he began to reproach the Romans for their faithlessness to the Goths and upbraided them for the treason which he said they had committed against both their fatherland and themselves, for they had exchanged the power of the Goths for Greeks who were not able to defend them, although they had never before seen any men of the Greek race come to Italy except actors of tragedy and mimes and thieving sailors.[94] Such words and many like them were spoken by Vacis, but since no one replied to him, he returned to the Goths and Vittigis. As for Belisarius, he brought upon himself much ridicule on the part of the Romans, for though he had barely escaped from the enemy, he bade them take courage thenceforth and look with contempt upon the barbarians; for he knew well, he said, that he would conquer them decisively. Now the manner in which he had come to know this with certainty will be told in the following narrative.[95] At length, when it was well on in the night, Belisarius, who had been fasting up to this time, was with difficulty compelled by his wife and those of his friends who were present to taste a very little bread. Thus, then, the two armies passed this night.

[185]

WALLS AND GATES OF
ROME
IN THE VI. CENTURY A.D.
Scale of Yards
0 500 1000 1500
Campus Neronis
VATICAN HILL
Basilica of St. Peter
Tomb of Hadrian
Porta Cornelia
Campus Martius
Porta Flaminia
Porta Pinciana
PINCIAN HILL
Via Flaminia
Via Pinciana
Porta Salaria
Porta Nomentana
Via Nomentana
QUIRINAL HILL
VIMINAL HILL
ESQUILINE HILL
Oppian Hill
Via Tiburtina
Porta Tiburtina
Via Praenestina
Via Labicana
Porta Praenestina
Porta Labicana
CAPITOLINE HILL
PALATINE HILL
CAELIAN HILL
Porta Asinaria
Via Asinaria
Porta Metrovia
Porta Latina
Via Latina
Via Appia
Porta Appia
AVENTINE HILL
Porta Ostiensis
Via Ostiensis
TIBER RIVER
Via Portuensis
Porta Portuensis
MONS JANICULEUM
Via Septimiana
Via Tecta
Via Aurelia
Porta Aurelia
Sancti Pancratii
Janiculum Arx
Gothic Camp

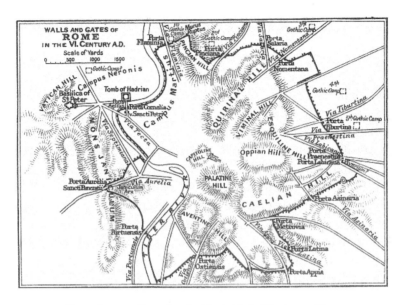

Based upon the plan in Hodgkin's "Italy and her Invaders." *Edward Stanford Ltd. London*

FOOTNOTES:

[89] Having a white spot, "White-face."

[90] See plan opposite p. 185.

[91] See plan opposite p. 185.

[92] For Procopius' description of the wall "across the Tiber," see chap. xix. 6-10.

[93] See plan opposite p. 185.

[94] Cf. Book IV. xxvii. 38, note.

[95] Chap. xxvii. 25-29.

XIX

But on the following day they arrayed themselves for the struggle, the Goths thinking to capture Rome by siege without any trouble on account of the great size of the city, and the Romans defending it. Now the wall of the city has fourteen large gates and several smaller ones. And the Goths, being unable with their entire army to envelop the wall on every side, made six fortified camps from which they harassed the portion of the wall containing five gates, from the Flaminian as far as the one called the Praenestine Gate; and all these camps were made by them on the left bank of the Tiber River. Wherefore the barbarians feared lest their enemy, by destroying the bridge which bears the name of Mulvius, should render inaccessible to them all the land on the right bank of the river as far as the sea, and in this way have not the slightest experience of the evils of a siege, and so they fixed a seventh camp across the Tiber in the Plain of Nero, in order that the bridge might be between their two armies. So in this way two other gates came to be exposed to the attacks of the enemy, the Aurelian[96] (which is now named after Peter, the chief of the Apostles of Christ, since he lies not far from there[97]) and the Transtiburtine Gate.[98] Thus the Goths surrounded only about one-half of the wall with their army, but since they were in no direction wholly shut off from the wall by the river, they made attacks upon [187]it throughout its whole extent whenever they wished.

Now the way the Romans came to build the city-wall on both sides of the river I shall now proceed to tell. In ancient times the Tiber used to flow alongside the circuit-wall for a considerable distance, even at the place where it is now enclosed. But this ground, on which the wall rises along the stream of the river, is flat and very accessible. And opposite this flat ground, across the Tiber, it happens that there is a great hill[99] where all the mills of the city have been built from of old, because much water is brought by an aqueduct to the crest of the hill, and rushes thence down the incline with great force. For this reason the ancient Romans[100] determined to surround the hill and the river bank near it with a wall, so that it might never be possible for an enemy to destroy the mills, and crossing the river, to carry on operations with ease against the circuit-wall of the city. So they decided to span the river at this point with a bridge, and to attach it to the wall; and by building many houses in the district across the river they caused the stream of the Tiber to be in the middle of the city. So much then for this.

And the Goths dug deep trenches about all their camps, and heaped up the earth, which they took out from them, on the inner side of the trenches, making this bank exceedingly high, and they planted great numbers of sharp stakes on the top, [189]thus making all their camps in no way inferior to fortified strongholds. And the camp in the Plain of Nero was commanded by Marcias (for he had by now arrived from Gaul with his followers, with whom he was encamped there), and the rest of the camps were commanded by Vittigis with five others; for there was one commander for each camp. So the Goths, having taken their positions in this way, tore open all the aqueducts, so that no water at all might enter the city from them. Now the aqueducts of Rome are fourteen in number, and were made of baked brick by the men of old, being of such breadth and height that it is possible for a man on horseback to ride in them.[101] And Belisarius arranged for the defence of the city in the following manner. He himself held the small Pincian Gate and the gate next to this on the right, which is named the Salarian. For at these gates the circuit-wall was assailable, and at the same time it was possible for the Romans to go out from them against the enemy. The Praenestine Gate he gave to Bessas. And at the Flaminian, which is on the other side of the Pincian, he put Constantinus in command, having previously closed the gates and blocked them up most securely by building a wall of great stones on the inside, so that it might be impossible for anyone to open them. For since one of the camps was very near, he feared least some secret plot against the city should be made there by the enemy. And the remaining gates he ordered the commanders of the infantry forces to keep under guard. And he closed each of the aqueducts as securely as possible by filling their channels with masonry for a consider[191]able distance, to prevent anyone from entering through them from the outside to do mischief.

But after the aqueducts had been broken open, as I have stated, the water no longer worked the mills, and the Romans were quite unable to operate them with any kind of animals owing to the scarcity of all food in time of siege; indeed they were scarcely able to provide for the horses which were indispensable to them. And so Belisarius hit upon the following device. Just below the bridge[102] which I lately mentioned as being connected with the circuit-wall, he fastened ropes from the two banks of the river and stretched them as tight as he could, and then attached to them two boats side by side and two feet apart, where the flow of the water comes down from the arch of the bridge with the greatest force, and placing two mills on either boat, he hung between them the mechanism by which mills are customarily turned. And below these he fastened other boats, each attached to the one next behind in order, and he set the water-wheels between them in the same manner for a great distance. So by the force of the flowing water all the wheels, one after the other, were made to revolve independently, and thus they worked the mills with which they were connected and ground sufficient flour for the city. Now when the enemy learned this from the deserters, they destroyed the wheels in the following manner. They gathered large trees and bodies of Romans newly slain and kept throwing them into the river; and the most of these were carried with the current between the boats and broke off the mill-wheels. But Belisarius, observing what was being [193]done, contrived the following device against it. He fastened above the bridge long iron chains, which reached completely across the Tiber. All the objects which the river brought down struck upon these chains, and gathered there and went no farther. And those to whom this work was assigned kept pulling out these objects as they came and bore them to the land. And Belisarius did this, not so much on account of the mills, as because he began to think with alarm that the enemy might get inside the bridge at this point with many boats and be in the middle of the city before their presence became known. Thus the barbarians abandoned the attempt, since they met with no success in it. And thereafter the Romans continued to use these mills; but they were entirely excluded from the baths because of the scarcity of water. However, they had sufficient water to drink, since even for those who lived very far from the river it was possible to draw water from wells. But as for the sewers, which carry out from the city whatever is unclean, Belisarius was not forced to devise any plan of safety, for they all discharge into the Tiber River, and therefore it was impossible for any plot to be made against the city by the enemy in connection with them.

FOOTNOTES:

[96] This is an error. Procopius means the Porta Cornelia.

[97] According to tradition the Basilica of St. Peter was built over the grave of the Apostle.

[98] The Aurelian.

[99] The Janiculum.

[100] The wall described was a part of the wall of Aurelian.

[101] This is an exaggeration; the channels vary from four to eight feet in height.

[102] The Pons Aurelius. See section 10 of this chapter.

XX

Thus, then, did Belisarius make his arrangements for the siege. And among the Samnites a large company of children, who were pasturing flocks in [195]their own country, chose out two among them who were well favoured in strength of body, and calling one of them by the name of Belisarius, and naming the other Vittigis, bade them wrestle. And they entered into the struggle with the greatest vehemence and it so fell out that the one who impersonated Vittigis was thrown. Then the crowd of boys in play hung him to a tree. But a wolf by some chance appeared there, whereupon the boys all fled, and the one called Vittigis, who was suspended from the tree, remained for some time suffering this punishment and then died. And when this became known to the Samnites, they did not inflict any punishment upon these children, but divining the meaning of the incident declared that Belisarius would conquer decisively. So much for this.

But the populace of Rome were entirely unacquainted with the evils of war and siege. When, therefore, they began to be distressed by their inability to bathe and the scarcity of provisions, and found themselves obliged to forgo sleep in guarding the circuit-wall, and suspected that the city would be captured at no distant date; and when, at the same time, they saw the enemy plundering their fields and other possessions, they began to be dissatisfied and indignant that they, who had done no wrong, should suffer siege and be brought into peril of such magnitude. And gathering in groups by themselves, they railed openly against Belisarius, on the ground that he had dared to take the field against the Goths before he had received an adequate force from the emperor. And these reproaches against Belisarius were secretly indulged in also by the members of the council which [197]they call the senate. And Vittigis, hearing all this from the deserters and desiring to embroil them with one another still more, and thinking that in this way the affairs of the Romans would be thrown into great confusion, sent to Belisarius some envoys, among whom was Albis. And when these men came before

Belisarius, they spoke as follows in the presence of the Roman senators and all the commanders of the army:

"From of old, general, mankind has made true and proper distinctions in the names they give to things; and one of these distinctions is this—rashness is different from bravery. For rashness, when it takes possession of a man, brings him into danger with discredit, but bravery bestows upon him an adequate prize in reputation for valour. Now one of these two has brought you against us, but which it is you will straightway make clear. For if, on the one hand, you placed your confidence in bravery when you took the field against the Goths, there is ample opportunity, noble sir, for you to do the deeds of a brave man, since you have only to look down from your wall to see the army of the enemy; but if, on the other hand, it was because you were possessed by rashness that you came to attack us, certainly you now repent you of the reckless undertaking. For the opinions of those who have made a desperate venture are wont to undergo a change whenever they find themselves in serious straits. Now, therefore, do not cause the sufferings of these Romans to be prolonged any further, men whom Theoderic fostered in a life not only of soft luxury but also of freedom, and cease your resistance to him who is the master both of the Goths and of the Italians. Is it not monstrous that you [199]should sit in Rome hemmed in as you are and in abject terror of the enemy, while the king of this city passes his time in a fortified camp and inflicts the evils of war upon his own subjects? But we shall give both you and your followers an opportunity to take your departure forthwith in security, retaining all your possessions. For to trample upon those who have learned to take a new view of prudence we consider neither holy nor worthy of the ways of men. And, further, we should gladly ask these Romans what complaints they could have had against the Goths that they betrayed both us and themselves, seeing that up to this time they have enjoyed our kindness, and now are acquainted by experience with the assistance to be expected from you."

Thus spoke the envoys. And Belisarius replied as follows: "It is not to rest with you to choose the moment for conference. For men are by no means wont to wage war according to the judgment of their enemies, but it is customary for each one to arrange his own affairs for himself, in whatever manner seems to him best. But I say to you that there will come a time when you will want to hide your heads under the thistles but will find no shelter anywhere. As for Rome, moreover, which we have captured, in holding it we hold nothing which belongs to others, but it was you who trespassed upon this city in former times, though it did not belong to you at all, and now you have given it back, however unwillingly, to its ancient possessors. And whoever of you has hopes of setting foot in Rome without a fight is mistaken in his judgment. For as long as Belisarius lives, it is impossible for him to relinquish this city." Such were the words of Belisarius. But the Romans, [201]being overcome by a great fear, sat in silence, and, even though they were abused by the envoys at length for their treason to the Goths, dared make no reply to them, except, indeed, that Fidelius saw fit to taunt them. This man was then praetorian prefect, having been appointed to the office by Belisarius, and for this reason he seemed above all others to be well disposed toward the emperor.

XXI

The envoys then betook themselves to their own army. And when Vittigis enquired of them what manner of man Belisarius was and how his purpose stood with regard to the question of withdrawing from Rome, they replied that the Goths were hoping for vain things if they supposed that they would frighten Belisarius in any way whatsoever. And when Vittigis heard this, he began in great earnest to plan an assault upon the wall, and the preparations he made for the attempt upon the fortifications were as follows. He constructed wooden towers equal in height to the enemy's wall, and he discovered its true measure by making many calculations based upon the courses of stone. And wheels were attached to the floor of these towers under each corner, which were intended, as they turned, to move the towers to any point the attacking army might wish at a given time, and the towers were drawn by oxen yoked together. After this he made ready a great number of ladders, that would reach as far as the parapet, and four engines which are called rams. Now this [203]engine is of the following sort. Four upright wooden beams, equal in length, are set up opposite one another. To these beams they fit eight horizontal timbers, four above and an equal number at the base, thus binding them together. After they have thus made the frame of a four-sided building, they surround it on all sides, not with walls of wood or stone, but with a covering of hides, in order that the engine may be light for those who draw it and that those within may still be in the least possible danger of being shot by their opponents. And on the inside they hang another horizontal beam from the top by means of chains which swing free, and they keep it at about the middle of the interior. They then sharpen the end of this beam and cover it with a large iron head, precisely as they cover the round point of a missile, or they sometimes make the iron head square like an anvil. And the whole structure is raised upon four wheels, one being attached to each upright beam, and men to the number of no fewer than fifty to each ram move it from the inside. Then when they apply it to the wall, they draw back the beam which I have just mentioned by turning a certain mechanism, and then they let it swing forward with great force against the wall. And this beam by frequent blows is able quite easily to batter down and tear open a wall wherever it strikes, and it is for this reason that the engine has the name it bears, because the striking end of the beam, projecting as it does, is accustomed to butt against whatever it may encounter, precisely as do the males among sheep. Such, then, are the rams used by the assailants of a wall. And the Goths were holding in readiness an exceedingly great number of bundles of faggots, [205]which they had made of pieces of wood and reeds, in order that by throwing them into the moat they might make the ground level, and that their engines might not be prevented from crossing it. Now after the Goths had made their preparations in this manner, they were eager to make an assault upon the wall.

But Belisarius placed upon the towers engines which they call "ballistae."[103] Now these engines have the form of a bow, but on the under side of them a grooved wooden shaft projects; this shaft is so fitted to the bow that it is free to move, and rests upon a straight iron bed. So when men wish to shoot at the enemy with this, they make the parts of the bow which form the ends bend toward one another by means of a short rope fastened to them, and they place in the grooved shaft the arrow, which is about one half the length of the ordinary missiles which they shoot from bows, but about four times as wide. However, it does not have feathers of the usual sort attached to it, but by inserting thin pieces of wood in place of feathers, they give it in all respects the form of an arrow, making the point which they put on very large and in keeping with its thickness. And the men who stand on either side wind it up tight by means of certain appliances, and then the grooved shaft shoots forward and stops, but the missile is discharged from the shaft,[104] and with such force that it [207]attains the distance of not less than two bow-shots, and that, when it hits a tree or a rock, it pierces it easily. Such is the engine which bears this name, being so called because it shoots with very great force.[105] And they fixed other engines along the parapet of the wall adapted for throwing stones. Now these resemble slings and are called "wild asses."[106] And outside the gates they placed "wolves,"[107] which they make in the following manner. They set up two timbers which reach from the ground to the battlements; then they fit together beams which have been mortised to one another, placing some upright and others crosswise, so that the spaces between the intersections appear as a succession of holes. And from every joint there projects a kind of beak, which resembles very closely a thick goad. Then they fasten the cross-beams to the two upright timbers, beginning at the top and letting them extend half way down, and then lean the timbers back against the gates. And whenever the enemy come up near them, those above lay hold of the ends of the timbers and push, and these, falling suddenly upon the assailants, easily kill with the projecting beaks as many as they may catch. So Belisarius was thus engaged.

FOOTNOTES:

[209]

[103] Cf. The description of the ballista and other engines of war in Ammianus Marcellinus, XXII. iv. The engine here described by Procopius is the catapult of earlier times; the ballista hurled stones, not arrows. See the Classical Dictionaries for illustrations.

[104]The "shaft" is a holder for the missile, and it (not the missile) is driven by the bowstring. When the holder stops, the missile goes on.

[105]A popular etymology of ἀλλιστρα, a corrupted form of βάλλιςτα; the point is in the Greek words βάλλω + μάλιστα, an etymology correct only as far as βάλλω is concerned.

[106] Called also "scorpions"; described by Ammianus, *l.c.*

[107] This contrivance was not one familiar to classical times. The "lupi" of Livy XXVIII. iii. were hooks; Vegetius, *De Re Militari*, ii. 25 and iv. 23, mentions "lupi" (also hooks), used to put a battering-ram out of action.

XXII

On the eighteenth day from the beginning of the siege the Goths moved against the fortifications at about sunrise under the leadership of Vittigis in order to assault the wall, and all the Romans were struck with consternation at the sight of the advancing towers and rams, with which they were altogether unfamiliar. But Belisarius, seeing the ranks of the enemy as they advanced with the engines, began to laugh, and commanded the soldiers to remain quiet and under no circumstances to begin fighting until he himself should give the signal. Now the reason why he laughed he did not reveal at the moment, but later it became known. The Romans, however, supposing him to be hiding his real feelings by a jest, abused him and called him shameless, and were indignant that he did not try to check the enemy as they came forward. But when the Goths came near the moat, the general first of all stretched his bow and with a lucky aim hit in the neck and killed one of the men in armour who were leading the army on. And he fell on his back mortally wounded, while the whole Roman army raised an extraordinary shout such as was never heard before, thinking that they had received an excellent omen. And twice did Belisarius send forth his bolt, and the very same thing happened again a second time, and the shouting rose still louder from the circuit-wall, and the Romans thought that the enemy were conquered already. Then Belisarius gave the signal for the [211]whole army to put their bows into action, but those near himself he commanded to shoot only at the oxen. And all the oxen fell immediately, so that the enemy could neither move the towers further nor in their perplexity do anything to meet the emergency while the fighting was in progress. In this way the forethought of Belisarius in not trying to check the enemy while still at a great distance came to be understood, as well as the reason why he had laughed at the simplicity of the barbarians, who had been so thoughtless as to hope to bring oxen up to the enemy's wall. Now all this took place at the Salarian Gate. But Vittigis, repulsed at this point, left there a large force of Goths, making of them a very deep phalanx and instructing the commanders on no condition to make an assault upon the fortifications, but remaining in position to shoot rapidly at the parapet, and give Belisarius no opportunity whatever to take reinforcements to any other part of the wall which he himself might propose to attack with a superior force; he then went to the Praenestine Gate with a great force, to a part of the fortifications which the Romans call the "Vivarium,"[108] where the wall was most assailable. Now it so happened that engines of war were already there, including towers and rams and a great number of ladders.

But in the meantime another Gothic assault was being made at the Aurelian Gate[109] in the following manner. The tomb of the Roman Emperor Hadrian[110] stands outside the Aurelian Gate, removed about a stone's throw from the fortifications, a very note[213]worthy sight. For it is made of Parian marble, and the stones fit closely one upon the other, having nothing at all[111] between them. And it has four sides which are all equal, each being about a stone's throw in length, while their height exceeds that of the city wall; and above there are statues of the same marble, representing men and horses, of wonderful workmanship.[112] But since this tomb seemed to the men of ancient times a fortress threatening the city, they enclosed it by two walls, which extend to it from the circuit-wall,[113] and thus made it a part of the wall. And, indeed, it gives the appearance of a high tower built as a bulwark before the gate there. So the fortifications at that point were most adequate. Now Constantinus, as it happened, had been appointed by Belisarius to have charge of the garrison at this tomb. And he had instructed him also to attend to the guarding of the adjoining wall, which had a small and inconsiderable garrison. For, since that part of the circuit-wall was the least assailable of all, because the river flows along it, he supposed that no assault would be made there, and so stationed an insignificant garrison at that place, and, since the soldiers he had were few, he assigned the great majority to the positions where there was most need of them. For the emperor's army gathered in Rome at the beginning of this siege amounted at most to [215]only five thousand men. But since it was reported to Constantinus that the enemy were attempting the crossing of the Tiber, he became fearful for that part of the fortifications and went thither himself with all speed, accompanied by some few men to lend assistance, commanding the greater part of his men to attend to the guarding of the gate and the tomb. But meanwhile the Goths began an assault upon the Aurelian Gate and the Tower of Hadrian, and though they had no engines of war, they brought up a great quantity of ladders, and thought that by shooting a vast number of arrows they would very easily reduce the enemy to a state of helplessness and overpower the garrison there without any trouble on account of its small numbers. And as they advanced, they held before them shields no smaller than the long shields used by the Persians, and they succeeded in getting very close to their opponents without being perceived by them. For they came hidden under the colonnade which extends[114] to the church of the Apostle Peter. From that shelter they suddenly appeared and began the attack, so that the guards were neither able to use the engine called the ballista (for these engines do not send their missiles except straight out), nor, indeed, could they ward off their assailants with their arrows, since the situation was against them on account of the large shields. But the Goths kept pressing vigorously upon them, shooting many missiles at the battlements, and they were already about to set their ladders against the wall, having practically surrounded those who were fighting from the tomb; for whenever the Goths advanced they always got in the rear of the Romans [217]on both flanks[115]; and for a short time consternation fell upon the Romans, who knew not what means of defence they should employ to save themselves, but afterwards by common agreement they broke in pieces the most of the statues, which were very large, and taking up great numbers of stones thus secured, threw them with both hands down upon the heads of the enemy, who gave way before this shower of missiles. And as they retreated a little way, the Romans, having by now the advantage, plucked up courage, and with a mighty shout began to drive back their assailants by using their bows and hurling stones at them. And putting their hands to the engines, they reduced their opponents to great fear, and their assault was quickly ended. And by this time Constantinus also was present, having frightened back those who had tried the river and easily driven them off, because they did not find the wall there entirely unguarded, as they had supposed they would. And thus safety was restored at the Aurelian Gate.[116]

FOOTNOTES:

[108] See chap. xxiii. 15-17 and note.

[109] Procopius errs again (cf. chap. xix. 4). He means the Porta Cornelia.

[110] Now called Castello di Sant' Angelo.

[111] *i.e.* No mortar or other binding material.

[112] The square structure was the base of the monument, each side measuring 300 Roman feet in length and 85 feet in height. Above this rose a cylindrical drum, surrounded by columns and carrying the statues, and perhaps capped by a second drum. For details see Jordan, *Topographie der Stadt Rom*, iii. 663 ff.

[113] Procopius neglects to say that the tomb was across the river from the circuit-wall at this point, at the end of a bridge (Pons Aelius) which faced the gate (Porta Cornelia) which he calls the Aurelian Gate.

[114] From the Pons Aelius.

[115] Because of the quadrangular shape of the building the Goths were able to take their enemy in flank and in rear by advancing beyond the corners.

[116] *i.e.* the Cornelian.

XXIII

But at the gate beyond the Tiber River, which is called the Pancratian Gate, a force of the enemy came, but accomplished nothing worth mentioning because of the strength of the place; for the fortifications of the city at this point are on a steep elevation and are not favourably situated for assaults. Paulus was keeping guard there with an infantry detachment which he commanded in person. In [219]like manner they made no attempt on the Flaminian Gate, because it is situated on a precipitous slope and is not very easy of access. The "Reges,"[117] an infantry detachment, were keeping guard there with Ursicinus, who commanded them. And between this gate and the small gate next on the right, which is called the Pincian, a certain portion of the wall had split open of its own accord in ancient times, not clear to the ground, however, but about half way down, but still it had not fallen or been otherwise destroyed, though it leaned so to either side that one part of it appeared outside the rest of the wall and the other inside. And from this circumstance the Romans from ancient times have called the place "Broken Wall"[118] in their own tongue. But when Belisarius in the beginning undertook to tear down this portion and rebuild it, the Romans prevented him, declaring that the Apostle Peter had promised them that he would care for the guarding of the wall there. This Apostle is reverenced by the Romans and held in awe above all others. And the outcome of events at this place was in all respects what the Romans contemplated and expected. For neither on that day nor throughout the whole time during which the Goths were besieging Rome did any hostile force come to that place, nor did any disturbance occur there. And we marvelled indeed that it never occurred to us nor to the enemy to remember this portion of the [221]fortifications during the whole time, either while they were making their assaults or carrying out their designs against the wall by night; and yet many such attempts were made. It was for this reason, in fact, that at a later time also no one ventured to rebuild this part of the defences, but up to the present day the wall there is split open in this way. So much, then, for this.

And at the Salarian Gate a Goth of goodly stature and a capable warrior, wearing a corselet and having a helmet on his head, a man who was of no mean station in the Gothic nation, refused to remain in the ranks with his comrades, but stood by a tree and kept shooting many missiles at the parapet. But this man by some chance was hit by a missile from an engine which was on a tower at his left. And passing through the corselet and the body of the man, the missile sank more than half its length into the tree, and pinning him to the spot where it entered the tree, it suspended him there a corpse. And when this was seen by the Goths they fell into great fear, and getting outside the range of missiles, they still remained in line, but no longer harassed those on the wall.

But Bessas and Peranius summoned Belisarius, since Vittigis was pressing most vigorously upon them at the Vivarium. And he was fearful concerning the wall there (for it was most assailable at that point, as has been said[119]), and so came to the rescue himself with all speed, leaving one of his friends at [223]the Salarian Gate. And finding that the soldiers in the Vivarium dreaded the attack of the enemy, which was being pressed with great vigour and by very large numbers, he bade them look with contempt upon the enemy and thus restored their confidence. Now the ground there[120] was very level, and consequently the place lay open to the attacks of any assailant. And for some reason the wall at that point had crumbled a great deal, and to such an extent that the binding of the bricks did not hold together very well. Consequently the ancient Romans had built another wall of short length outside of it and encircling it, not for the sake of safety (for it was neither strengthened with towers, nor indeed was there any battlement built upon it, nor any other means by which it would have been possible to repulse an enemy's assault upon the fortifications), but in order to provide for an unseemly kind of luxury, namely, that they might confine and keep there lions and other wild animals. And it is for this reason that this place has been named the Vivarium; for thus the Romans call a place where untamed animals are regularly cared for. So Vittigis began to make ready various engines at different places along the wall and commanded the Goths to mine the outside wall, thinking that, if they should get inside that, they would have no trouble in capturing the main wall, which he knew to be by no means strong. But Belisarius, seeing that the enemy was undermining the Vivarium and assaulting the fortifications at many places, neither [225]allowed the soldiers to defend the wall nor to remain at the battlement, except a very few, although he had with him whatever men of distinction the army contained. But he held them all in readiness below about the gates, with their corselets on and carrying only swords in their hands. And when the Goths, after making a breach in the wall, got inside the Vivarium, he quickly sent Cyprian with some others into the enclosure against them, commanding them to set to work. And they slew all who had broken in, for these made no defence and at the same time were being destroyed by one another in the cramped space about the exit. And since the enemy were thrown into dismay by the sudden turn of events and were not drawn up in order, but were rushing one in one direction and one in another, Belisarius suddenly opened the gates of the circuit-wall and sent out his entire army against his opponents. And the Goths had not the least thought of resistance, but rushed off in flight in any and every direction, while the Romans, following them up, found no difficulty in killing all whom they fell in with, and the pursuit proved a long one, since the Goths, in assaulting the wall at that place, were far away from their own camps. Then Belisarius gave the order to burn the enemy's engines, and the flames, rising to a great height, naturally increased the consternation of the fugitives.

Meanwhile it chanced that the same thing happened at the Salarian Gate also. For the Romans suddenly opened the gates and fell unexpectedly upon the barbarians, and, as these made no resistance but turned their backs, slew them; and they [227]burned the engines of war which were within their reach. And the flames at many parts of the wall rose to a great height, and the Goths were already being forced to retire from the whole circuit-wall; and the shouting on both sides was exceedingly loud, as the men on the wall urged on the pursuers, and those in the camps bewailed the overwhelming calamity they had suffered. Among the Goths there perished on that day thirty thousand, as their leaders declared, and a larger number were wounded; for since they were massed in great numbers, those fighting from the battlement generally hit somebody when they shot at them, and at the same time those who made the sallies destroyed an extraordinary number of terrified and fleeing men. And the fighting at the wall, which had commenced early in the morning, did not end until late in the afternoon. During that night, then, both armies bivouacked where they were, the Romans singing the song of victory on the fortifications and lauding Belisarius to the skies, having with them the spoils stripped from the fallen, while the Goths cared for their wounded and bewailed their dead.

FOOTNOTES:

[117] "No doubt these are the same as the *Regii*, one of the seventeen 'Auxilia Palatina' under the command of the Magister Militum Praesentalis, mentioned in the *Notitia Orientis*, chap. v."—HODGKIN.

[118] Murus Ruptus. "Here, to this day, notwithstanding some lamentable and perfectly unnecessary 'restorations' of recent years, may be seen some portions of the Muro Torto, a twisted, bulging, overhanging mass of *opus reticulatum*."—HODGKIN.

[119] Chap. xxii. 10.

[120] The exact location is hard to determine; the majority of the authorities agree on the location given in the plan (opposite p. 185), near the Porta Labicana.

XXIV

And Belisarius wrote a letter to the emperor of the following purport: "We have arrived in Italy, as thou didst command, and we have made ourselves masters of much territory in it and have taken possession of Rome also, after driving out the barbarians who were here, whose leader, Leuderis, I have recently sent to you. But since we have stationed [229]a great number of soldiers both in Sicily and in Italy to guard the strongholds which we have proved able to capture, our army has in consequence been reduced to only five thousand men. But the enemy have come against us, gathered together to the number of one hundred and fifty thousand. And first of all, when we went out to spy upon their forces along the Tiber River and were compelled, contrary to our intention, to engage with them, we lacked only a little of being buried under a multitude of spears. And after this, when the barbarians attacked the wall with their whole army and assaulted the fortifications at every point with sundry engines of war, they came within a little of capturing both us and the city at the first onset, and they would have succeeded had not some chance snatched us from ruin. For achievements which transcend the nature of things may not properly and fittingly be ascribed to man's valour, but to a stronger power. Now all that has been achieved by us hitherto, whether it has been due to some kind fortune or to valour, is for the best; but as to our prospects from now on, I could wish better things for thy cause. However, I shall never hide from you anything that it is my duty to say and yours to do, knowing that while human affairs follow whatever course may be in accordance with God's will, yet those who are in charge of any enterprise always win praise or blame according to their own deeds. Therefore let both arms and soldiers be sent to us in such numbers that from now on we may engage with the enemy in this war with an equality of strength. For one ought not to trust everything to fortune, since fortune, on its part, is not given to following the same course [231]forever. But do thou, O Emperor, take this thought to heart, that if at this time the barbarians win the victory over us, we shall be cast out of Italy which is thine and shall lose the army in addition, and besides all this we shall have to bear the shame, however great it may be, that attaches to our conduct. For I refrain from saying that we should also be regarded as having ruined the Romans, men who have held their safety more lightly than their loyalty to thy kingdom. Consequently, if this should happen, the result for us will be that the successes we have won thus far will in the end prove to have been but a prelude to calamities. For if it had so happened that we had been repulsed from Rome and Campania and, at a much earlier time, from Sicily, we should only be feeling the sting of the lightest of all misfortunes, that of having found ourselves unable to grow wealthy on the possessions of others. And again, this too is worthy of consideration by you, that it has never been possible even for many times ten thousand men to guard Rome for any considerable length of time, since the city embraces a large territory, and, because it is not on the sea, is shut off from all supplies. And although at the present time the Romans are well disposed toward us, yet when their troubles are prolonged, they will probably not hesitate to choose the course which is better for their own interests. For when men have entered into friendship with others on the spur of the moment, it is not while they are in evil fortune, but while they prosper, that they are accustomed to keep faith with them. Furthermore, the Romans will be compelled by hunger to do many things they would prefer not to do.[233] Now as for me, I know I am bound even to die for thy kingdom, and for this reason no man will ever be able to remove me from this city while I live; but I beg thee to consider what kind of a fame such an end of Belisarius would bring thee."

Such was the letter written by Belisarius. And the emperor, greatly distressed, began in haste to gather an army and ships, and sent orders to the troops of Valerian and Martinus[121] to proceed with all speed. For they had been sent, as it happened, with another army at about the winter solstice, with instructions to sail to Italy. But they had sailed as far as Greece, and since they were unable to force their way any farther, they were passing the winter in the land of Aetolia and Acarnania. And the Emperor Justinian sent word of all this to

Belisarius, and thus filled him and all the Romans with still greater courage and confirmed their zeal.

At this time it so happened that the following event took place in Naples. There was in the market-place a picture of Theoderic, the ruler of the Goths, made by means of sundry stones which were exceedingly small and tinted with nearly every colour. At one time during the life of Theoderic it had come to pass that the head of this picture fell apart, the stones as they had been set having become disarranged without having been touched by anyone, and by a coincidence Theoderic finished his life forthwith. And eight years later the stones which formed the body of the picture fell apart suddenly, and Atalaric, the grandson of Theoderic, immediately died. And after the passage of a short time, the [235]stones about the groin fell to the ground, and Amalasuntha, the child of Theoderic, passed from the world. Now these things had already happened as described. But when the Goths began the siege of Rome, as chance would have it, the portion of the picture from the thighs to the tips of the feet fell into ruin, and thus the whole picture disappeared from the wall. And the Romans, divining the meaning of the incident, maintained that the emperor's army would be victorious in the war, thinking that the feet of Theoderic were nothing else than the Gothic people whom he ruled, and, in consequence, they became still more hopeful.

In Rome, moreover, some of the patricians brought out the Sibylline oracles,[122] declaring that the danger which had come to the city would continue only up till the month of July. For it was fated that at that time someone should be appointed king over the Romans, and thenceforth Rome should have no longer any Getic peril to fear; for they say that the Goths are of the Getic race. And the oracle was as follows: "In the fifth (Quintilis) month . . . under . . . as king nothing Getic longer. . . ." And they declared that the "fifth month" was July, some because the siege began on the first day of March, from which July is the fifth month, others because March was considered the first month until the reign of Numa, the full year before that time containing ten months and our July for this reason

[237]having its name Quintilis. But after all, none of these predictions came true. For neither was a king appointed over the Romans at that time, nor was the siege destined to be broken up until a year later, and Rome was again to come into similar perils in the reign of Totila, ruler of the Goths, as will be told by me in the subsequent narrative.[123] For it seems to me that the oracle does not indicate this present attack of the barbarians, but some other attack which has either happened already or will come at some later time. Indeed, in my opinion, it is impossible for a mortal man to discover the meaning of the Sibyl's oracles before the actual event. The reason for this I shall now set forth, having read all the oracles in question. The Sibyl does not invariably mention events in their order, much less construct a well-arranged narrative, but after uttering some verse or other concerning the troubles in Libya she leaps straightway to the land of Persia, thence proceeds to mention the Romans, and then transfers the narrative to the Assyrians. And again, while uttering prophecies about the Romans, she foretells the misfortunes of the Britons. For this reason it is impossible for any man soever to comprehend the oracles of the Sibyl before the event, and it is only time itself, after the event has already come to pass and the words can be tested by experience, that can shew itself an accurate interpreter of her sayings. But as for these things, let each one reason as he desires. But I shall return to the point from which I have strayed.

FOOTNOTES:

[121] Leaders of foederati; see Book III. xi. 4-6; they had been recalled from Africa to Byzantium, cf. Book IV. xix. 2.

[122] The story of the origin of these oracles is given in Dionysius of Halicarnassus, *Ant. Rom.* IV. lxii. They were burned with the Capitol in 83 B.C. The second collection was burned by Stilicho in 405 A.D. The oracles Procopius saw (cf. § 35 of this chapter) were therefore a third collection.

[123] Book VII. xx.

[239]

XXV

When the Goths had been repulsed in the fight at the wall, each army bivouacked that night in the manner already described.[124] But on the following day Belisarius commanded all the Romans to remove their women and children to Naples, and also such of their domestics as they thought would not be needed by them for the guarding of the wall, his purpose being, naturally, to forestall a scarcity of provisions. And he issued orders to the soldiers to do the same thing, in case anyone had a male or female attendant. For, he went on to say, he was no longer able while besieged to provide them with food to the customary amount, but they would have to accept one half their daily ration in actual supplies, taking the remainder in silver. So they proceeded to carry out his instructions. And immediately a great throng set out for Campania. Now some, who had the good fortune to secure such boats as were lying at anchor in the harbour[125] of Rome, secured passage, but the rest went on foot by the road which is called the Appian Way. And no danger or fear, as far as the besiegers were concerned, arose to disturb either those who travelled this way on foot or those who set out from the harbour. For, on the one hand, the enemy were unable to surround the whole of Rome with their camps on account of the great size of the city, and, on the other, they did not dare to be found far from the camps in small [241]companies, fearing the sallies of their opponents. And on this account abundant opportunity was afforded for some time to the besieged both to move out of the city and to bring provisions into it from outside. And especially at night the barbarians were always in great fear, and so they merely posted guards and remained quietly in their camps. For parties were continually issuing from the city, and especially Moors in great numbers, and whenever they found their enemies either asleep or walking about in small companies (as is accustomed to happen often in a large army, the men going out not only to attend to the needs of nature, but also to pasture horses and mules and such animals as are suitable for food), they would kill them and speedily strip them, and if perchance a larger number of the enemy should fall upon them, they would retire on the run, being men swift of foot by nature and lightly equipped, and always distancing their pursuers in the flight. Consequently, the great majority were able to withdraw from Rome, and some went to Campania, some to Sicily, and others wherever they thought it was easier or better to go. But Belisarius saw that the number of soldiers at his command was by no means sufficient for the whole circuit of the wall, for they were few, as I have previously stated,[126] and the same men could not keep guard constantly without sleeping, but some would naturally be taking their sleep while others were stationed on guard. At the same time he saw that the greatest part of the populace were hard pressed by poverty and in want of the necessities of life; [243]for since they were men who worked with their hands, and all they had was what they got from day to day, and since they had been compelled to be idle on account of the siege, they had no means of procuring provisions. For these reasons Belisarius mingled soldiers and citizens together and distributed them to each post, appointing a certain fixed wage for an unenlisted man for each day. In this way companies were made up which were sufficient for the guarding of the wall, and the duty of keeping guard on the fortifications during a stated night was assigned to each company, and the members of the companies all took turns in standing guard. In this manner, then, Belisarius did away with the distress of both soldiers and citizens.

But a suspicion arose against Silverius, the chief priest of the city, that he was engaged in treasonable negotiations with the Goths, and Belisarius sent him immediately to Greece, and a little later appointed another man, Vigilius by name, to the office of chief priest. And he banished from Rome on the same charge some of the senators, but later, when the enemy had abandoned the siege and retired, he restored them again to their homes. Among these was Maximus, whose ancestor Maximus[127] had committed the crime against the Emperor Valentinian. And fearing lest the guards at the gates should become involved in a plot, and lest someone should gain access from the outside with intent to corrupt them with money, twice in each month he destroyed all the keys and had new ones made, each time of a different design, and he also changed the guards to other posts which were far removed from those they [245]had formerly occupied, and every night he set different men in charge of those who were doing guard-duty on the fortifications. And it was the duty of these officers to make the rounds of a section of the wall, taking turns in this work, and to write down the names of the guards, and if anyone was missing from that section, they put another man on duty in his stead for the moment, and on the morrow reported the missing man to Belisarius himself, whoever he might be, in order that the fitting punishment might be given him. And he ordered musicians to play their instruments on the fortifications at night, and he continually sent detachments of soldiers, especially Moors, outside the walls, whose duty it was always to pass the night about the moat, and he sent dogs with them in order that no one might approach the fortifications, even at a distance, without being detected.

At that time some of the Romans attempted secretly to force open the doors of the temple of Janus. This Janus was the first of the ancient gods whom the Romans call in their own tongue "Penates."[128] And he has his temple in that part of the forum in front of the senate-house which lies a little above the "Tria Fata"[129]; for thus the Romans are accustomed to call the Moirai.[130] And the temple is entirely of bronze and was erected in the form of a square, but it is only large enough to cover the statue of Janus. Now this statue, is of bronze, and [247]not less than five cubits high; in all other respects it resembles a man, but its head has two faces, one of which is turned toward the east and the other toward the west. And there are brazen doors fronting each face, which the Romans in olden times were accustomed to close in time of peace and prosperity, but when they had war they opened them. But when the Romans came to honour, as truly as any others, the teachings of the Christians, they gave up the custom of opening these doors, even when they were at war. During this siege, however, some, I suppose, who had in mind the old belief, attempted secretly to open them, but they did not succeed entirely, and moved the doors only so far that they did not close tightly against one another as formerly. And those who had attempted to do this escaped detection; and no investigation of the act was made, as was natural in a time of great confusion, since it did not become known to the commanders, nor did it reach the ears of the multitude, except of a very few.

FOOTNOTES:

[124] Chap. xxiii. 27.

[125] At this time the town of Portus, on the north side of the Tiber's mouths, Ostia, on the south side, having been long neglected. Cf. chap. xxvi. 7, 8.

[126] Five thousand; cf. chap. xxiv. 2.

[127] Book III. iv. 36.

[128] Janus was an old Italian divinity, whose worship was said to have been introduced by Romulus. We are not told by anyone else that he was included among the Penates, but the statement is doubtless true.

[129] "This temple of Janus—the most celebrated, but not the only one in Rome—must have stood a little to the right of the Arch of Septimius Severus (as one looks toward the Capitol) and a little in front of the Mamertine Prison."—HODGKIN. The "Tria Fata" were three ancient statues of Sibyls which stood by the Rostra.

[130] *i.e.* the Fates.

XXVI

Now Vittigis, in his anger and perplexity, first sent some of his bodyguards to Ravenna with orders to kill all the Roman senators whom he had taken there at the beginning of this war. And some of them, learning of this beforehand, succeeded in making their escape, among them being Vergentinus and Reparatus, the brother of Vigilius, the chief priest of Rome, both of whom betook them[249]selves into Liguria and remained there; but all the rest were destroyed. After this Vittigis, seeing that the enemy were enjoying a large degree of freedom, not only in taking out of the city whatever they wished, but also in bringing in provisions both by land and by sea, decided to seize the harbour, which the Romans call "Portus."

This harbour is distant from the city one hundred and twenty-six stades; for Rome lacks only so much of being on the sea; and it is situated where the Tiber River has its mouth.[131] Now as the Tiber flows down from Rome, and reaches a point rather near the sea, about fifteen stades from it, the stream divides into two parts and makes there the Sacred Island, as it is called. As the river flows on the island becomes wider, so that the measure of its breadth corresponds to its length, for the two streams have between them a distance of fifteen stades; and the Tiber remains navigable on both sides. Now the portion of the river on the right empties into the harbour, and beyond the mouth the Romans in ancient times built on the shore a city,[132] which is surrounded by an exceedingly strong wall; and it is called, like the harbour, "Portus." But on the left at the point where the other part of the Tiber empties into the sea is situated the city of Ostia, lying beyond the place where the river-bank ends, a place of great consequence in olden times, but now entirely without walls. Moreover, the Romans [251]at the very beginning made a road leading from Portus to Rome, which was smooth and presented no difficulty of any kind. And many barges are always anchored in the harbour ready for service, and no small number of oxen stand in readiness close by. Now when the merchants reach the harbour with their ships, they unload their cargoes and place them in the barges, and sail by way of the Tiber to Rome; but they do not use sails or oars at all, for the boats cannot be propelled in the stream by any wind since the river winds about exceedingly and does not follow a straight course, nor can oars be employed, either, since the force of the current is always against them. Instead of using such means, therefore, they fasten ropes from the barges to the necks of oxen, and so draw them just like waggons up to Rome. But on the other side of the river, as one goes from the city of Ostia to Rome, the road is shut in by woods and in general lies neglected, and is not even near the bank of the Tiber, since there is no towing of barges on that road.

So the Goths, finding the city at the harbour unguarded, captured it at the first onset and slew many of the Romans who lived there, and so took possession of the harbour as well as the city. And they established a thousand of their number there as guards, while the remainder returned to the camps. In consequence of this move it was impossible for the besieged to bring in the goods which came by sea, except by way of Ostia, a route which naturally involved great labour and danger besides. For the[253] Roman ships were not even able to put in there any longer, but they anchored at Anthium,[133] a day's journey distant from Ostia. And they found great difficulty in carrying the cargoes thence to Rome, the reason for this being the scarcity of men. For Belisarius, fearing for the fortifications of Rome, had been unable to strengthen the harbour with any garrison at all, though I think that if even three hundred men had been on guard there, the barbarians would never have made an attempt on the place, which is exceedingly strong.

FOOTNOTES:

[131] The northern mouth.

[132] The Emperor Claudius cut the northern channel for the river, in order to prevent inundations of Rome, and made the "Portus Claudii,"

opening to the sea, near its mouth; a second enclosed harbour, adjoining that of Claudius, was built by Trajan.

[133] *i.e.* Antium.

XXVII

This exploit, then, was accomplished by the Goths on the third day after they were repulsed in the assault on the wall. But twenty days after the city and harbour of Portus were captured, Martinus and Valerian arrived, bringing with them sixteen hundred horsemen, the most of whom were Huns and Sclaveni[134] and Antae,[135] who are settled above the Ister River not far from its banks. And Belisarius was pleased by their coming and thought that thenceforth his army ought to carry the war against the enemy. On the following day, accordingly, he commanded one of his own bodyguards, Trajan by name, an impetuous and active fighter, to take two hundred horsemen of the guards and go straight towards the enemy, and as soon as they came near the camps to go up on a high hill (which he pointed out to him)[255] and remain quietly there. And if the enemy should come against them, he was not to allow the battle to come to close quarters, nor to touch sword or spear in any case, but to use bows only, and as soon as he should find that his quiver had no more arrows in it, he was to flee as hard as he could with no thought of shame and retire to the fortifications on the run. Having given these instructions, he held in readiness both the engines for shooting arrows and the men skilled in their use. Then Trajan with the two hundred men went out from the Salarian Gate against the camp of the enemy. And they, being filled with amazement at the suddenness of the thing, rushed out from the camps, each man equipping himself as well as he could. But the men under Trajan galloped to the top of the hill which Belisarius had shewn them, and from there began to ward off the barbarians with missiles. And since their shafts fell among a dense throng, they were for the most part successful in hitting a man or a horse. But when all their missiles had at last failed them, they rode off to the rear with all speed, and the Goths kept pressing upon them in pursuit. But when they came near the fortifications, the operators of the engines began to shoot arrows from them, and the barbarians became terrified and abandoned the pursuit. And it is said that not less than one thousand Goths perished in this action. A few days later Belisarius sent Mundilas, another of his own bodyguard, and Diogenes, both exceptionally capable warriors, with three hundred guardsmen, [257]commanding them to do the same thing as the others had done before. And they acted according to his instructions. Then, when the enemy confronted them, the result of the encounter was that no fewer than in the former action, perhaps even more, perished in the same way. And sending even a third time the guardsman Oilas with three hundred horsemen, with instructions to handle the enemy in the same way, he accomplished the same result. So in making these three sallies, in the manner told by me, Belisarius destroyed about four thousand of his antagonists.

But Vittigis, failing to take into account the difference between the two armies in point of equipment of arms and of practice in warlike deeds, thought that he too would most easily inflict grave losses upon the enemy, if only he should make his attack upon them with a small force. He therefore sent five hundred horsemen, commanding them to go close to the fortifications, and to make a demonstration against the whole army of the enemy of the very same tactics as had time and again been used against them, to their sorrow, by small bands of the foe. And so, when they came to a high place not far from the city, but just beyond the range of missiles, they took their stand there. But Belisarius selected a thousand men, putting Bessas in command, and ordered them to engage with the enemy. And this force, by forming a circle around the enemy and always shooting at them from behind, killed a large number, and by pressing hard upon the rest compelled them to descend into the plain. There a hand-to-hand battle took place between forces not evenly matched in strength, and most of the Goths were destroyed, though some few with difficulty [259]made their escape and returned to their own camp. And Vittigis reviled these men, insisting that cowardice had been the cause of their defeat, and undertaking to find another set of men to retrieve the loss after no long time, he remained quiet for the present; but three days later he selected men from all the camps, five hundred in number, and bade them make a display of valorous deeds against the enemy. Now as soon as Belisarius saw that these men had come rather near, he sent out against them fifteen hundred men under the commanders Martinus and Valerian. And a cavalry battle taking place immediately, the Romans, being greatly superior to the enemy in numbers, routed them without any trouble and destroyed practically all of them.

And to the enemy it seemed in every way a dreadful thing and a proof that fortune stood against them, if, when they were many and the enemy who came against them were few, they were defeated, and when, on the other hand, they in turn went in small numbers against their enemy, they were likewise destroyed. Belisarius, however, received a public vote of praise from the Romans for his wisdom, at which they not unnaturally marvelled greatly, but in private his friends asked him on what he had based his judgment on that day when he had escaped from the enemy after being so completely defeated,[136] and why he had been confident that he would overcome them decisively in the war. And he said that in engaging with them at the first with only a few men he had noticed just what the difference was between the two armies, so [261]that if he should fight his battles with them with a force which was in strength proportionate to theirs,[137] the multitudes of the enemy could inflict no injury upon the Romans by reason of the smallness of their numbers. And the difference was this, that practically all the Romans and their allies, the Huns, are good mounted bowmen, but not a man among the Goths has had practice in this branch, for their horsemen are accustomed to use only spears and swords, while their bowmen enter battle on foot and under cover of the heavy-armed men. So the horsemen, unless the engagement is at close quarters, have no means of defending themselves against opponents who use the bow, and therefore can easily be reached by the arrows and destroyed; and as for the foot-soldiers, they can never be strong enough to make sallies against men on horseback. It was for these reasons, Belisarius declared, that the barbarians had been defeated by the Romans in these last engagements. And the Goths, remembering the unexpected outcome of their own experiences, desisted thereafter from assaulting the fortifications of Rome in small numbers and also from pursuing the enemy when harassed by them, except only so far as to drive them back from their own camps.

FOOTNOTES:

[134] *i.e.* Slavonians, described in Book VI. xxvi. and Book VII. xiv. ff.

[135] A Slavic people, described in Book VII. xiv.

[136] Referring to the battle described in chap. xviii.

[137] *i.e.* smaller, but equal in strength.

XXVIII

But later on the Romans, elated by the good fortune they had already enjoyed, were with one accord eager to do battle with the whole Gothic army and thought that they should make war in the open field.[263] Belisarius, however, considering that the difference in size of the two armies was still very great, continued to be reluctant to risk a decisive battle with his whole army; and so he busied himself still more with his sallies and kept planning them against the enemy. But when at last he yielded his point because of the abuse heaped upon him by the army and the Romans in general, though he was willing to fight with the whole army, yet nevertheless he wished to open the engagement by a sudden sally. And many times he was frustrated when he was on the point of doing this, and was compelled to put off the attack to the following day, because he found to his surprise that the enemy had been previously informed by deserters as to what was to be done and were unexpectedly ready for him. For this reason, then, he was now willing to fight a decisive battle even in the open field, and the barbarians gladly came forth for the encounter. And when both sides had been made ready for the conflict as well as might be, Belisarius gathered his whole army and exhorted them as follows:

"It is not because I detected any cowardice on your part, fellow-soldiers, nor because I was terrified at the strength of the enemy, that I have shrunk from the engagement with them, but I saw that while we were carrying on the war by making sudden sallies matters stood well with us, and consequently I thought that we ought to adhere permanently to the tactics which were responsible for our success. For I think that when one's present affairs are going to one's satisfaction, it is inexpedient to change to another course of action. But since I see that you are eager for this danger, I am filled with con[265]fidence and shall never oppose your ardour. For I know that the greatest factor in the decision of war is always the attitude of the fighting men, and it is generally by their enthusiasm that successes are won. Now, therefore, the fact that a few men drawn up for battle with valour on their side are able to overcome a multitude of the enemy, is well known by every man of you, not by hearsay, but by daily experience of fighting. And it will rest with you not to bring shame upon the former glories of my career as general, nor upon the hope which this enthusiasm of yours inspires. For the whole of what has already been accomplished by us in this war must of necessity be judged in accordance with the issue of the present day. And I see that the present moment is also in our favour, for it will, in all probability, make it easier for us to gain the mastery over the enemy, because their spirit has been enslaved by what has gone before. For when men have often met with misfortune, their hearts are no longer wont to thrill even slightly with manly valour. And let no one of you spare horse or bow or any weapon. For I will immediately provide you with others in place of all that are destroyed in the battle."

After speaking these words of exhortation, Belisarius led out his army through the small Pincian Gate and the Salarian Gate, and commanded some few men to go through the Aurelian Gate into the Plain of Nero. These he put under the command of Valentinus, a commander of a cavalry detachment, and he directed him not to begin any fighting, or to go too close to the camp of the enemy, but constantly to give the appearance of being [267]about to attack immediately, so that none of the enemy in that quarter might be able to cross the neighbouring bridge and come to the assistance of the soldiers from the other camps. For since, as I have previously stated,[138] the barbarians encamped in the Plain of Nero were many, it seemed to him sufficient if these should all be prevented from taking part in the engagement and be kept separated from the rest of the army. And when some of the Roman populace took up arms and followed as volunteers, he would not allow them to be drawn up for battle along with the regular troops, fearing lest, when they came to actual fighting, they should become terrified at the danger and throw the entire army into confusion, since they were labouring men and altogether unpractised in war. But outside the Pancratian Gate, which is beyond the Tiber River, he ordered them to form a phalanx and remain quiet until he himself should give the signal, reasoning, as actually proved to be the case, that if the enemy in the Plain of Nero should see both them and the men under Valentinus, they would never dare leave their camp and enter battle with the rest of the Gothic army against his own forces. And he considered it a stroke of good luck and a very important advantage that such a large number of men should be kept apart from the army of his opponents.

Such being the situation, he wished on that day to engage in a cavalry battle only; and indeed most of the regular infantry were now unwilling to remain in their accustomed condition, but, since they had captured horses as booty from the enemy and had become not unpractised in horsemanship, they were [269]now mounted. And since the infantry were few in number and unable even to make a phalanx of any consequence, and had never had the courage to engage with the barbarians, but always turned to flight at the first onset, he considered it unsafe to draw them up at a distance from the fortifications, but thought it best that they should remain in position where they were, close by the moat, his purpose being that, if it should so happen that the Roman horsemen were routed, they should be able to receive the fugitives and, as a fresh body of men, help them to ward off the enemy.

But there were two men among his bodyguards, a certain Principius, who was a man of note and a Pisidian by birth, and Tarmutus, an Isaurian, brother of Ennes who was commander of the Isaurians. These men came before Belisarius and spoke as follows: "Most excellent of generals, we beg you neither to decide that your army, small as it is and about to fight with many tens of thousands of barbarians, be cut off from the phalanx of the infantry, nor to think that one ought to treat with contumely the infantry of the Romans, by means of which, as we hear, the power of the ancient Romans was brought to its present greatness. For if it so happens that they have done nothing of consequence in this war, this is no evidence of the cowardice of the soldiers, but it is the commanders of the infantry who would justly bear the blame, for they alone ride on horseback in the battle-line and are not willing to consider the fortunes of war as shared by all, but as a general thing each one of them by himself takes to flight before the struggle begins. But do you keep all the commanders of [271]infantry, since you see that they have become cavalry and that they are quite unwilling to take their stand beside their subordinates, and include them with the rest of the cavalry and so enter this battle, but permit us to lead the infantry into the combat. For since we also are unmounted, as are these troops, we shall do our part in helping them to support the attack of the multitude of barbarians, full of hope that we shall inflict upon the enemy whatever chastisement God shall permit."

When Belisarius heard this request, at first he did not assent to it; for he was exceedingly fond of these two men, who were fighters of marked excellence, and he was unwilling to have a small body of infantry take such a risk. But finally, overborne by the eagerness of the men, he consented to leave only a small number of their soldiers, in company with the Roman populace, to man the gates and the battlement along the top of the wall where the engines of war were, and to put the rest under command of Principius and Tarmutus, ordering them to take position in the rear in regular formation. His purpose in this was, in the first place, to keep these troops from throwing the rest of the army into confusion if they themselves should become panic-stricken at the danger, and, in the second place, in case any division of the cavalry should be routed at any time, to prevent the retreat from extending to an indefinite distance, but to allow the cavalry simply to fall back upon the infantry and make it possible for them, with the infantry's help, to ward off the pursuers.[273]

FOOTNOTE:

[138] Chap. xix. 12, xiii. 15.

XXIX

In this fashion the Romans had made their preparations for the encounter. As for Vittigis, he had armed all the Goths, leaving not a man behind in the camps, except those unfit for fighting. And he commanded the men under Marcias to remain in the Plain of Nero, and to attend to the guarding of the bridge, that the enemy might not attack his men from that direction. He himself then called together the rest of the army and spoke as follows:

"It may perhaps seem to some of you that I am fearful about my sovereignty, and that this is the motive which has led me, in the past, to shew a friendly spirit toward you and, on the present occasion, to address you with seductive words in order to inspire you with courage. And such reasoning is not out of accord with the ways of men. For unenlightened men are accustomed to shew gentleness toward those whom they want to make use of, even though these happen to be in a much humbler station than they, but to be difficult of access to others whose assistance they do not desire. As for me, however, I care neither for the end of life nor for the loss of power. Nay, I should even pray that I might put off this purple to-day, if a Goth were to put it on. And I have always regarded the end of Theodatus as one of the most fortunate, in that he was privileged to lose both his sovereignty and his life at the hands of men of his own nation. For a calamity which falls upon an individual without involving his nation also in destruction does not lack an element of consolation, in the view, at least, of men who are not wanting in [275]wisdom. But when I reflect upon the fate of the Vandals and the end of Gelimer, the thoughts which come to my mind are of no ordinary kind; nay, I seem to see the Goths and their children reduced to slavery, your wives ministering in the most shameful of all ways to the most hateful of men, and myself and the granddaughter[139] of Theoderic led wherever it suits the pleasure of those who are now our enemies; and I would have you also enter this battle fearing lest this fate befall us. For if you do this, on the field of battle you will count the end of life as more to be desired than safety after defeat. For noble men consider that there is only one misfortune—to survive defeat at the hands of their enemy. But as for death, and especially death which comes quickly, it always brings happiness to those who were before not blest by fortune. It is very clear that if you keep these thoughts in mind as you go through the present engagement, you will not only conquer your opponents most easily, few as they are and Greeks,[140] but will also punish them forthwith for the injustice and insolence with which they, without provocation, have treated us. For although we boast that we are their superiors in valour, in numbers, and in every other respect, the boldness which they feel in confronting us is due merely to elation at our misfortunes; and the only asset they have is the indifference we have shewn. For their self-confidence is fed by their undeserved good fortune."

With these words of exhortation Vittigis proceeded to array his army for battle, stationing the infantry in the centre and the cavalry on the two wings. He did not, however, draw up his phalanx far from the [277]camps, but very near them, in order that, as soon as the rout should take place, the enemy might easily be overtaken and killed, there being abundance of room for the pursuit. For he expected that if the struggle should become a pitched battle in the plain, they would not withstand him even a short time; since he judged by the great disparity of numbers that the army of the enemy was no match for his own.

So the soldiers on both sides, beginning in the early morning, opened battle; and Vittigis and Belisarius were in the rear urging on both armies and inciting them to fortitude. And at first the Roman arms prevailed, and the barbarians kept falling in great numbers before their archery, but no pursuit of them was made. For since the Gothic cavalry stood in dense masses, other men very easily stepped into the places of those who were killed, and so the loss of those who fell among them was in no way apparent. And the Romans evidently were satisfied, in view of their very small number, that the struggle should have such a result for them. So after they had by midday carried the battle as far as the camps of their opponents, and had already slain many of the enemy, they were anxious to return to the city if any pretext should present itself to them. In this part of the action three among the Romans proved themselves brave men above all others, Athenodorus, an Isaurian, a man of fair fame among the guards of Belisarius, and Theodoriscus and George, spearmen of Martinus and Cappadocians by birth. For they constantly kept going out beyond the front of the phalanx, and there [279]despatched many of the barbarians with their spears. Such was the course of events here.

But in the Plain of Nero the two armies remained for a long time facing one another, and the Moors, by making constant sallies and hurling their javelins among the enemy, kept harrying the Goths. For the Goths were quite unwilling to go out against them through fear of the forces of the Roman populace which were not far away, thinking, of course, that they were soldiers and were remaining quiet because they had in mind some sort of an ambush against themselves with the object of getting in their rear, exposing them to attack on both sides, and thus destroying them. But when it was now the middle of the day, the Roman army suddenly made a rush against the enemy, and the Goths were unexpectedly routed, being paralyzed by the suddenness of the attack. And they did not succeed even in fleeing to their camp, but climbed the hills near by and remained quiet. Now the Romans, though many in number, were not all soldiers, but were for the most part a throng of men without defensive armour. For inasmuch as the general was elsewhere, many sailors and servants in the Roman camp, in their eagerness to have a share in the war, mingled with that part of the army. And although by their mere numbers they did fill the barbarians with consternation and turn them to flight, as has been said, yet by reason of their lack of order they lost the day for the Romans. For the intermixture of the above-mentioned men caused the soldiers to be thrown into great disorder, and although Valentinus kept constantly shouting orders to them, they could not hear his commands at all. For this reason they did not even follow up the [281]fugitives or kill a man, but allowed them to stand at rest on the hills and in security to view what was going on. Nor did they take thought to destroy the bridge there, and thus prevent the city from being afterwards besieged on both sides; for, had they done so, the barbarians would have been unable to encamp any longer on the farther side of the Tiber River. Furthermore, they did not even cross the bridge and get in the rear of their opponents who were fighting there with the troops of Belisarius. And if this had been done, the Goths, I think, would no longer have thought of resistance, but they would have turned instantly to flight, each man as he could. But as it was, they took possession of the enemy's camp and turned to plundering his goods, and they set to work carrying thence many vessels of silver and many other valuables. Meanwhile the barbarians for some time remained quietly where they were and observed what was going on, but finally by common consent they advanced against their opponents with great fury and shouting. And finding men in complete disorder engaged in plundering their property, they slew many and quickly drove out the rest. For all who were caught inside the camp and escaped slaughter were glad to cast their plunder from their shoulders and take to flight.

While these things were taking place in the Plain of Nero, meantime the rest of the barbarian army stayed very near their camps and, protecting themselves with their shields, vigorously warded off their opponents, destroying many men and a much larger number of horses. But on the Roman side, when those who had been wounded and those whose horses had [283]been killed left the ranks, then, in an army which had been small even before, the smallness of their numbers was still more evident, and the difference between them and the Gothic host was manifestly great. Finally the horsemen of the barbarians who were on the right wing, taking note of this, advanced at a gallop against the enemy opposite them. And the Romans there, unable to withstand their spears, rushed off in flight and came to the infantry phalanx. However, the infantry also were unable to hold their ground against the oncoming horsemen, and most of them began to join the cavalry in flight. And immediately the rest of the Roman army also began to retire, the enemy pressing upon their heels, and the rout became decisive. But Principius and Tarmutus with some few of the infantry of their command made a display of valorous deeds against the Goths. For as they continued to fight and disdained to turn to flight with the others, most of the Goths were so amazed that they halted. And consequently the rest of the infantry and most of the horsemen made their escape in greater security. Now Principius fell where he stood, his whole body hacked to pieces, and around him fell forty-two foot-soldiers. But Tarmutus, holding two Isaurian javelins, one in each hand, continued to thrust them into his assailants as he turned from side to side, until, finally, he desisted because his body was covered with wounds; but when his brother Ennes came to the rescue with a detachment of cavalry, he revived, and running swiftly, covered as he was with gore and wounds, he made for the fortifications without throwing down either of his javelins. And being fleet of foot by [285]nature, he succeeded in making his escape, in spite of the plight of his body, and did not fall until he had just reached the Pincian Gate. And some of his comrades, supposing him to be dead, lifted him on a shield and carried him. But he lived on two days before he died, leaving a high reputation both among the Isaurians and in the rest of the army.

The Romans, meanwhile, being by now thoroughly frightened, attended to the guarding of the wall, and shutting the gates they refused, in their great excitement, to receive the fugitives into the city, fearing that the enemy would rush in with them. And such of the fugitives as had not already got inside the fortifications, crossed the moat, and standing with their backs braced against the wall were trembling with fear, and stood there forgetful of all valour and utterly unable to ward off the barbarians, although they were pressing upon them and were about to cross the moat to attack them. And the reason was that most of them had lost their spears, which had been broken in the engagement and during the flight, and they were not able to use their bows because they were huddled so closely together. Now so long as not many defenders were seen at the battlement, the Goths kept pressing on, having hopes of destroying all those who had been shut out and of overpowering the men who held the circuit-wall. But when they saw a very great number both of soldiers and of the Roman populace at the battlements defending the wall, they immediately abandoned their purpose and rode off thence to the rear, heaping much abuse upon their opponents. And the battle, having begun at the camps of the barbarians, ended at the moat and the wall of the city.[287]

FOOTNOTES:

[139] Matasuntha.

[140] Cf. Book IV. xxvii. 38, note.

[289]

HISTORY OF THE WARS:

BOOK VI

THE GOTHIC WAR (*continued*)

I

After this the Romans no longer dared risk a battle with their whole army; but they engaged in cavalry battles, making sudden sallies in the same manner as before, and were generally victorious over the barbarians. Foot-soldiers also went out from both sides, not, however, arrayed in a phalanx, but accompanying the horsemen. And once Bessas in the first rush dashed in among the enemy carrying his spear and killed three of their best horsemen and turned the rest to flight. And another time, when Constantinus had led out the Huns in the Plain of Nero in the late afternoon, and saw that they were being overpowered by the superior numbers of their opponents, he took the following measures. There has been in that place from of old a great stadium[141] where the gladiators of the city used to fight in former times, and the men of old built many other buildings round about this stadium; consequently there are, as one would expect, narrow passages all about this place. Now on the occasion in question, since Constantinus could neither overcome the throng of the Goths nor flee without great danger, he caused [291]all the Huns to dismount from their horses, and on foot, in company with them, took his stand in one of the narrow passages there. Then by shooting from that safe position they slew large numbers of the enemy. And for some time the Goths withstood their missiles. For they hoped, as soon as the supply of missiles in the quivers of the Huns should be exhausted, to be able to surround them without any trouble, take them prisoners, and lead them back to their camp. But since the Massagetae, who were not only good bowmen but also had a dense throng to shoot into, hit an enemy with practically every shot, the Goths perceived that above half their number had perished, and since the sun was about to set, they knew not what to do and so rushed off in flight. Then indeed many of them fell; for the Massagetae followed them up, and since they know how to shoot the bow with the greatest accuracy even when running at great speed, they continued to discharge their arrows no less than before, shooting at their backs, and kept up the slaughter. And thus Constantinus with his Huns came back to Rome at night.

And when Peranius, not many days later, led some of the Romans through the Salarian Gate against the enemy, the Goths, indeed, fled as hard as they could, but about sunset a counter-pursuit was made suddenly, and a Roman foot-soldier, becoming greatly confused, fell into a deep hole, many of which were made there by the men of old, for the storage of grain, I suppose. And he did not dare to cry out, [293]supposing that the enemy were encamped near by, and was not able in any way whatever to get out of the pit, for it afforded no means of climbing up; he was therefore compelled to pass the night there. Now on the next day, when the barbarians had again been put to flight, one of the Goths fell into the same hole. And there the two men were reconciled to mutual friendship and good-will, brought together as they were by their necessity, and they exchanged solemn pledges, each that he would work earnestly for the salvation of the other; and then both of them began shouting with loud and frantic cries. Now the Goths, following the sound, came and peered over the edge of the hole, and enquired who it was who shouted. At this, the Roman, in accordance with the plan decided upon by the two men, kept silence, and the Goth in his native tongue said that he had just recently fallen in there during the rout which had taken place, and asked them to let down a rope that he might come up. And they as quickly as possible threw down the ends of ropes, and, as they thought, were pulling up the Goth, but the Roman laid hold of the ropes and was pulled up, saying only that if he should go up first the Goths would never abandon their comrade, but if they should learn that merely one of the enemy was there they would take no account of him. So saying, he went up. And when the Goths saw him, they wondered and were in great perplexity, but upon hearing the whole story from him they drew up his comrade next, and he told them of the agreement [295]they had made and of the pledges both had given. So he went off with his companions, and the Roman was released unharmed and permitted to return to the city. After this horsemen in no great numbers armed themselves many times for battle, but the struggles always ended in single combats, and the Romans were victorious in all of them. Such, then, was the course of these events.

A little after this an engagement took place in the Plain of Nero, wherein various small groups of horsemen were engaged in pursuing their opponents in various directions; in one group was Chorsamantis, a man of note among the guards of Belisarius, by birth a Massagete, who with some others was pursuing seventy of the enemy. And when he had got well out in the plain the other Romans rode back, but Chorsamantis went on with the pursuit alone. As soon as the Goths perceived this, they turned their horses about and came against him. And he advanced into their midst, killed one of the best of them with his spear, and then went after the others, but they again turned and rushed off in flight. But they were ashamed before their comrades in the camp, who, they suspected, could already see them, and wished to attack him again. They had, however, precisely the same experience as before and lost one of their best men, and so turned to flight in spite of their shame, and after Chorsamantis had pursued them as far as their stockade he returned alone. And a little later, in another battle, this man was wounded in the left shin, and it was his [297]opinion that the weapon had merely grazed the bone. However, he was rendered unfit for fighting for a certain number of days by reason of this wound, and since he was a barbarian he did not endure this patiently, but threatened that he would right speedily have vengeance upon the Goths for this insult to his leg. So when not long afterwards he had recovered and was drunk at lunch time, as was his custom, he purposed to go alone against the enemy and avenge the insult to his leg; and when he had come to the small Pincian Gate he stated that he was sent by Belisarius to the enemy's camp. And the guards at the gate, who could not doubt the word of a man who was the best of the guards of Belisarius, opened the gates and allowed him to go wherever he would. And when the enemy spied him, they thought at first that some deserter was coming over to them, but when he came near and put his hand to his bow, twenty men, not knowing who he might be, went out against him. These he easily drove off, and then began to ride back at a walk, and when more Goths came against him he did not flee. But when a great throng gathered about him and he still insisted upon fighting them, the Romans, watching the sight from the towers, suspected that the man was crazy, but they did not yet know that it was Chorsamantis. At length, after making a display of great and very noteworthy deeds, he found himself surrounded by the army of the enemy, and paid the penalty for his unreasonable daring. And when Belisarius and the Roman army learned this, they mourned greatly, lamenting that the hope which all placed in the man had come to naught.[299]

FOOTNOTE:

[141] Perhaps the Stadium of Caligula.

II

Now a certain Euthalius, at about the spring equinox, came to Taracina from Byzantium with the money which the emperor owed the soldiers. And fearing lest the enemy should come upon him on the road and both rob him of the money and kill him, he wrote to Belisarius requesting him to make the journey to Rome safe for him. Belisarius accordingly selected one hundred men of note from among his own bodyguards and sent them with two spearmen to Taracina to assist him in bringing the money. And at the same time he kept trying to make the barbarians believe that he was about to fight with his whole army, his purpose being to prevent any of the enemy from leaving the vicinity, either to bring in provisions or for any other purpose. But when he found out that Euthalius and his men would arrive on the morrow, he arrayed his army and set it in order for battle, and the barbarians were in readiness. Now throughout the whole forenoon he merely held his soldiers near the gates; for he knew that Euthalius and those who accompanied him would arrive at night. Then, at midday, he commanded the army to take their lunch, and the Goths did the same thing, supposing that he was putting off the engagement to the following day. A little later, however, Belisarius sent Martinus and Valerian to the Plain of Nero with the troops under their command, directing them to throw the enemy's camp into the [301]greatest possible confusion. And from the small Pincian Gate he sent out six hundred horsemen against the camps of the barbarians, placing them under command of three of his own spearmen, Artasires, a Persian, and Bochas, of the race of the Massagetae, and Cutilas, a Thracian. And many of the enemy came out to meet them. For a long time, however, the battle did not come to close quarters, but each side kept retreating when the other advanced and making pursuits in which they quickly turned back, until it looked as if they intended to spend the rest of the day at this sort of thing. But as they continued, they began at last to be filled with rage against each other. The battle then settled down to a fierce struggle in which many of the best men on both sides fell, and support came up for each of the two armies, both from the city and from the camps. And when these fresh troops were mingled with the fighters the struggle became still greater. And the shouting which filled the city and the camps terrified the combatants. But finally the Romans by their valour forced back the enemy and routed them.

In this action Cutilas was struck in the middle of the head by a javelin, and he kept on pursuing with the javelin still embedded in his head. And after the rout had taken place, he rode into the city at about sunset together with the other survivors, the javelin in his head waving about, a most extraordinary sight. During the same encounter Arzes, one of the guards of Belisarius, was hit by one of the Gothic [303]archers between the nose and the right eye. And the point of the arrow penetrated as far as the neck behind, but it did not shew through, and the rest of the shaft projected from his face and shook as the man rode. And when the Romans saw him and Cutilas they marvelled greatly that both men continued to ride, paying no heed to their hurt. Such, then, was the course of events in that quarter.

But in the Plain of Nero the barbarians had the upper hand. For the men of Valerian and Martinus, fighting with a great multitude of the enemy, withstood them stoutly, to be sure, but suffered most terribly, and came into exceedingly great danger. And then Belisarius commanded Bochas to take his troops, which had returned from the engagement unwearied, men as well as horses, and go to the Plain of Nero. Now it was already late in the day. And when the men under Bochas had come to the assistance of the Romans, suddenly the barbarians were turned to flight, and Bochas, who had impetuously followed the pursuit to a great distance, came to be surrounded by twelve of the enemy, who carried spears. And they all struck him at once with their spears. But his corselet withstood the other blows, which therefore did not hurt him much; but one of the Goths succeeded in hitting him from behind, at a place where his body was uncovered, above the right armpit, very close to the shoulder, and smote the youth, though not with a mortal stroke, nor even one which brought him into danger of death. But another Goth struck him in front and pierced his left thigh, and cut the muscles there; it was not a straight blow, however, but only a slanting cut. But Valerian and Martinus saw what [305]was happening, and coming to his rescue as quickly as possible, they routed the enemy, and both took hold of the bridle of Bochas' horse, and so came into the city. Then night came on and Euthalius entered the city with the money.

And when all had returned to the city, they attended to the wounded men. Now in the case of Arzes, though the physicians wished to draw the weapon from his face, they were for some time reluctant to do so, not so much on account of the eye, which they supposed could not possibly be saved, but for fear lest, by the cutting of membranes and tissues such as are very numerous in that region, they should cause the death of a man who was one of the best of the household of Belisarius. But afterwards one of the physicians, Theoctistus by name, pressed on the back of his neck and asked whether he felt much pain. And when the man said that he did feel pain, he said, "Then both you yourself will be saved and your sight will not be injured." And he made this declaration because he inferred that the barb of the weapon had penetrated to a point not far from the skin. Accordingly he cut off that part of the shaft which shewed outside and threw it away, and cutting open the skin at the back of the head, at the place where the man felt the most pain, he easily drew toward him the barb, which with its three sharp points now stuck out behind and brought with it the remaining portion of the weapon. Thus Arzes remained entirely free from serious harm, and not even a trace of his wound was left on his face. But as for Cutilas, when the javelin was drawn rather violently from his head (for it was very deeply [307]embedded), he fell into a swoon. And since the membranes about the wound began to be inflamed, he fell a victim to phrenitis[142] and died not long afterwards. Bochas, however, immediately had a very severe hemorrhage in the thigh, and seemed like one who was presently to die. And the reason for the hemorrhage, according to what the physicians said, was that the blow had severed the muscle, not directly from the front, but by a slanting cut. In any event he died three days later. Because of these things, then, the Romans spent that whole night in deep grief; while from the Gothic camps were heard many sounds of wailing and loud lamentation. And the Romans indeed wondered, because they thought that no calamity of any consequence had befallen the enemy on the previous day, except, to be sure, that no small number of them had perished in the encounters. This had happened to them before in no less degree, perhaps even to a greater degree, but it had not greatly distressed them, so great were their numbers. However, it was learned on the following day that men of the greatest note from the camp in the Plain of Nero were being bewailed by the Goths, men whom Bochas had killed in his first charge.

And other encounters also, though of no great importance, took place, which it has seemed to me unnecessary to chronicle. This, however, I will state, that altogether sixty-seven encounters occurred during this siege, besides two final ones which will be described in the following narrative. And at that time the winter drew to its close, and thus ended the second year of this war, the history of which Procopius has written.[309]

FOOTNOTE:

[142] Inflammation of the brain.

III

But at the beginning of the spring equinox famine and pestilence together fell upon the inhabitants of the city. There was still, it is true, some grain for the soldiers, though no other kind of provisions, but the grain-supply of the rest of the Romans had been exhausted, and actual famine as well as pestilence was pressing hard upon them. And the Goths, perceiving this, no longer cared to risk a decisive battle with their enemy, but they kept guard that nothing in future should be brought in to them. Now there are two aqueducts between the Latin and the Appian Ways, exceedingly high and carried on arches for a great distance. These two aqueducts meet at a place fifty stades distant from Rome[143] and cross each other, so that for a little space they reverse their relative position. For the one which previously lay to the right from then on continues on the left side. And again coming together, they resume their former places, and thereafter remain apart. Consequently the space between them, enclosed, as it is, by the aqueducts, comes to be a fortress. And the barbarians walled up the lower arches of the aqueducts here with stones and mud and in this way gave it the form of a fort, and encamping there to the number of no fewer than seven thousand men, they kept guard that no provisions should thereafter be brought into the city by the enemy. [311]

Then indeed every hope of better things abandoned the Romans, and every form of evil encompassed them round about. As long as there was ripe grain, however, the most daring of the soldiers, led on by lust of money, went by night to the grain-fields not far from the city mounted on horses and leading other horses after them. Then they cut off the heads of grain, and putting them on the horses which they led, would carry them into the city without being seen by the enemy and sell them at a great price to such of the Romans as were wealthy. But the other inhabitants lived on various herbs such as grow in abundance not only in the outskirts but also inside the fortifications. For the land of the Romans is never lacking in herbs either in winter or at any other season, but they always flourish and grow luxuriantly at all times. Wherefore the besieged also pastured their horses in those places. And some too made sausages of the mules that died in Rome and secretly sold them. But when the corn-lands had no more grain and all the Romans had come into an exceedingly evil plight, they surrounded Belisarius and tried to compel him to stake everything on a single battle with the enemy, promising that not one of the Romans would be absent from the engagement. And when he was at a loss what to do in that situation and greatly distressed, some of the populace spoke to him as follows:

"General, we were not prepared for the fortune which has overtaken us at the present time; on the contrary, what has happened has been altogether the opposite of our expectations. For after achieving what [313]we had formerly set our hearts upon, we have now come into the present misfortune, and we realize at length that our previous opinion that we did well to crave the emperor's watchful care was but folly and the beginning of the greatest evils. Indeed, this course has brought us to such straits that at the present time we have taken courage to use force once more and to arm ourselves against the barbarians. And while we may claim forgiveness if we boldly come into the presence of Belisarius—for the belly knows not shame when it lacks its necessities—our plight must be the apology for our rashness; for it will be readily agreed that there is no plight more intolerable for men than a life prolonged amid the adversities of fortune. And as to the fortune which has fallen upon us, you cannot fail to see our distress. These fields and the whole country have fallen under the hand of the enemy; and this city has been shut off from all good things for we know not how long a time. And as for the Romans, some already lie in death, and it has not been their portion to be hidden in the earth, and we who survive, to put all our terrible misfortunes in a word, only pray to be placed beside those who lie thus. For starvation shews to those upon whom it comes that all other evils can be endured, and wherever it appears it is attended by oblivion of all other sufferings, and causes all other forms of death, except that which proceeds from itself, to seem pleasant to men. Now, therefore, before the evil has yet mastered us, grant us leave on our own behalf to take up the struggle, which will result either in our overcoming the enemy or in deliverance [315]from our troubles. For when delay brings men hope of safety, it would be great folly for them prematurely to enter into a danger which involves their all, but when tarrying makes the struggle more difficult, to put off action even for a little time is more reprehensible than immediate and precipitate haste."

So spoke the Romans. And Belisarius replied as follows: "Well, as for me, I have been quite prepared for your conduct in every respect, and nothing that has happened has been contrary to my expectation. For long have I known that a populace is a most unreasoning thing, and that by its very nature it cannot endure the present or provide for the future, but only knows how rashly in every case to attempt the impossible and recklessly to destroy itself. But as for me, I shall never, willingly at least, be led by your carelessness either to destroy you or to involve the emperor's cause in ruin with you. For war is wont to be brought to a successful issue, not by unreasoning haste, but by the use of good counsel and forethought in estimating the turn of the scale at decisive moments. You, however, act as though you were playing at dice, and want to risk all on a single cast; but it is not my custom to choose the short course in preference to the advantageous one. In the second place, you promise that you will help us do battle against the enemy; but when have you ever taken training in war? Or who that has learned such things by the use of arms does not know that battle affords no room for experiment? Nor does the enemy, on his part, give opportunity, while the struggle is on, to practise on him. This [317]time, indeed, I admire your zeal and forgive you for making this disturbance; but that you have taken this action at an unseasonable time and that the policy of waiting which we are following is prudent, I shall now make clear. The emperor has gathered for us from the whole earth and despatched an army too great to number, and a fleet such as was never brought together by the Romans now covers the shore of Campania and the greater part of the Ionian Gulf. And within a few days these reinforcements will come to us and bring with them all kinds of provisions, to put an end to our destitution and to bury the camps of the barbarians under a multitude of missiles. I have therefore reasoned that it was better to put off the time of conflict until they are present, and thus gain the victory in the war with safety, than to make a show of daring in unreasoning haste and thus throw away the salvation of our whole cause. To secure their immediate arrival and to prevent their loitering longer shall be my concern."

FOOTNOTE:

[143] Torre Fiscale; but it is only about thirty stades from Rome.

IV

With these words Belisarius encouraged the Roman populace and then dismissed them; and Procopius, who wrote this history, he immediately commanded to go to Naples. For a rumour was going about that the emperor had sent an army there. And he commissioned him to load as many ships as possible with grain, to gather all the soldiers who at the moment had arrived from Byzantium, or had been left about Naples in charge of horses or for any other purpose whatever—for he had heard that many such were coming to the various places in[319] Campania—and to withdraw some of the men from the garrisons there, and then to come back with them, convoying the grain to Ostia, where the harbour of the Romans was. And Procopius, accompanied by Mundilas the guardsman and a few horsemen, passed out by night through the gate which bears the name of the Apostle Paul,[144] eluding the enemy's camp which had been established very close to the Appian Way to keep guard over it. And when Mundilas and his men, returning to Rome, announced that Procopius had already arrived in Campania without meeting any of the barbarians,—for at night, they said, the enemy never went outside their camp,—everybody became hopeful, and Belisarius, now emboldened, devised the following plan. He sent out many of his horsemen to the neighbouring strongholds, directing them, in case any of the enemy should come that way in order to bring provisions into their camps, that they should constantly make sallies upon them from their positions and lay ambushes everywhere about this region, and thus keep them from succeeding; on the contrary, they should with all their might hedge them in, so that the city might be in less distress than formerly through lack of provisions, and also that the barbarians might seem to be besieged rather than to be themselves besieging the Romans. So he commanded Martinus and Trajan with a thousand men to go to Taracina. And with them he sent also his wife Antonina, commanding that she be sent with a few men to Naples, there to await in safety the fortune which would befall the Romans. And he sent Magnus and Sinthues the guardsman, who took with them

[321]about five hundred men, to the fortress of Tibur, one hundred and forty stades distant from Rome. But to the town of Albani,[145] which was situated on the Appian Way at the same distance from the city, he had already, as it happened, sent Gontharis with a number of Eruli, and these the Goths had driven out from there by force not long afterward.

Now there is a certain church of the Apostle Paul,[146] fourteen stades distant from the fortifications of Rome, and the Tiber River flows beside it. In that place there is no fortification, but a colonnade extends all the way from the city to the church, and many other buildings which are round about it render the place not easy of access. But the Goths shew a certain degree of actual respect for sanctuaries such as this. And indeed during the whole time of the war no harm came to either church of the two Apostles[147] at their hands, but all the rites were performed in them by the priests in the usual manner. At this spot, then, Belisarius commanded Valerian to take all the Huns and make a stockade by the bank of the Tiber, in order that their horses might be kept in greater security and that the Goths might be still further checked from going at their pleasure to great distances from their camps. And Valerian acted accordingly. Then, after the Huns had made their camp in the place where the general directed, he rode back to the city.

So Belisarius, having accomplished this, remained quiet, not offering battle, but eager to carry on the defence from the wall, if anyone should advance [323]against it from outside with evil intent. And he also furnished grain to some of the Roman populace. But Martinus and Trajan passed by night between the camps of the enemy, and after reaching Taracina sent Antonina with a few men into Campania; and they themselves took possession of the fortified places in that district, and using them as their bases of operations and making thence their sudden attacks, they checked such of the Goths as were moving about in that region. As for Magnus and Sinthues, in a short time they rebuilt such parts of the fortress[148] as had fallen into ruin, and as soon as they had put themselves in safety, they began immediately to make more trouble for the enemy, whose fortress was not far away, not only by making frequent raids upon them, but also by keeping such of the barbarians as were escorting provision-trains in a constant state of terror by the unexpectedness of their movements; but finally Sinthues was wounded in his right hand by a spear in a certain battle, and since the sinews were severed, he became thereafter unfit for fighting. And the Huns likewise, after they had made their camp near by, as I have said, were on their part causing the Goths no less trouble, so that these as well as the Romans were now feeling the pressure of famine, since they no longer had freedom to bring in their food-supplies as formerly. And pestilence too fell upon them and was destroying many, and especially in the camp which they had last made, close by the Appian Way, as I have previously stated.[149] And the few of their number who had not perished withdrew from that camp to the other camps. The Huns also [325]suffered in the same way, and so returned to Rome. Such was the course of events here. But as for Procopius, when he reached Campania, he collected not fewer than five hundred soldiers there, loaded a great number of ships with grain, and held them in readiness. And he was joined not long afterwards by Antonina, who immediately assisted him in making arrangements for the fleet.

At that time the mountain of Vesuvius rumbled, and though it did not break forth in eruption, still because of the rumbling it led people to expect with great certainty that there would be an eruption. And for this reason it came to pass that the inhabitants fell into great terror. Now this mountain is seventy stades distant from Naples and lies to the north[150] of it—an exceedingly steep mountain, whose lower parts spread out wide on all sides, while its upper portion is precipitous and exceedingly difficult of ascent. But on the summit of Vesuvius and at about the centre of it appears a cavern of such depth that one would judge that it extends all the way to the bottom of the mountain. And it is possible to see fire there, if one should dare to peer over the edge, and although the flames as a rule merely twist and turn upon one another, occasioning no trouble to the inhabitants of that region, yet, when the mountain gives forth a rumbling sound which resembles bellowing, it generally sends up not long afterward a great quantity of ashes. And if anyone travelling on the road is caught by this terrible shower, he cannot possibly survive, and if it falls upon houses, they too fall under the weight of the great quantity of ashes. But whenever it so [327]happens that a strong wind comes on, the ashes rise to a great height, so that they are no longer visible to the eye, and are borne wherever the wind which drives them goes, falling on lands exceedingly far away. And once, they say, they fell in Byzantium[151] and so terrified the people there, that from that time up to the present the whole city has seen fit to propitiate God with prayers every year; and at another time they fell on Tripolis in Libya. Formerly this rumbling took place, they say, once in a hundred years or even more,[152] but in later times it has happened much more frequently. This, however, they declare emphatically, that whenever Vesuvius belches forth these ashes, the country round about is bound to flourish with an abundance of all crops. Furthermore, the air on this mountain is very light and by its nature the most favourable to health in the world. And indeed those who are attacked by consumption have been sent to this place by physicians from remote times. So much, then, may be said regarding Vesuvius.

FOOTNOTES:

[144] The Porta Ostiensis.

[145] See Book V. vi. 7, note.

[146] The Basilica of St. Paul stood south of the city, outside the Porta Ostiensis which is still called Porta S. Paolo.

[147] St. Peter and St. Paul.

[148] Tibur.

[149] Chap. iii. 7.

[150] This is an error on the part of Procopius. In point of fact it lies to the south-east of Naples.

[151] During the eruption of 472 A.D.

[152] Since the great eruption of 79 A.D.—the first in historical times—eruptions have succeeded one another at intervals varying from one to more than one hundred years.

V

At this time another army also arrived by sea from Byzantium, three thousand Isaurians who put in at the harbour of Naples, led by Paulus and Conon, and eight hundred Thracian horsemen who landed at Dryus, led by John, the nephew of the Vitalian who had formerly been tyrant, and with them a [329]thousand other soldiers of the regular cavalry, under various commanders, among whom were Alexander and Marcentius. And it happened that Zeno with three hundred horsemen had already reached Rome by way of Samnium and the Latin Way. And when John with all the others came to Campania, provided with many waggons by the inhabitants of Calabria, his troops were joined by five hundred men who, as I have said, had been collected in Campania. These set out by the coast road with the waggons, having in mind, if any hostile force should confront them, to make a circle of the waggons in the form of a stockade and thus to ward off the enemy; and they commanded the men under Paulus and Conon to sail with all speed and join them at Ostia, the harbour of Rome[153]; and they put sufficient grain in the waggons and loaded all the ships, not only with grain, but also with wine and all kinds of provisions. And they, indeed, expected to find the forces of Martinus and Trajan in the neighbourhood of Taracina and to have their company from that point on, but when they approached Taracina, they learned that these forces had recently been recalled and had retired to Rome.

But Belisarius, learning that the forces of John were approaching and fearing that the enemy might confront them in greatly superior numbers and destroy them, took the following measures. It so happened that the enemy had encamped very close to the Flaminian Gate; this gate Belisarius himself had blocked up at the beginning of this war by a [331]structure of stone, as has been told by me in the previous narrative,[154] his purpose of course being to make it difficult for the enemy either to force their way in or to make any attempt upon the city at that point. Consequently no engagement had taken place at this gate, and the barbarians had no suspicion that there would be any attack upon them from there. Now Belisarius tore down by night the masonry which blocked this gate, without giving notice to anyone at all, and made ready the greatest part of the army there. And at daybreak he sent Trajan and Diogenes with a thousand horsemen through the Pincian Gate, commanding them to shoot missiles into the camps, and as soon as their opponents came against them, to flee without the least shame and to ride up to the fortifications at full speed. And he also stationed some men inside this gate. So the men under Trajan began to harass the barbarians, as Belisarius had directed them to do, and the Goths, gathering from all the camps, began to defend themselves. And both armies began to move as fast as they could toward the fortifications of the city, the one giving the appearance of fleeing, and the other supposing that they were pursuing the enemy.

But as soon as Belisarius saw the enemy take up the pursuit, he opened the Flaminian Gate and sent his army out against the barbarians, who were thus taken unawares. Now it so happened that one of the Gothic camps was on the road near this gate, and in front of it there was a narrow passage between steep banks which was exceedingly difficult of access. And one of the barbarians, a man of splendid physique and clad in a corselet, when he saw the enemy [333]advancing, reached this place before them and took his stand there, at the same time calling his comrades and urging them to help in guarding the narrow passage. But before any move could be made Mundilas slew him and thereafter allowed none of the barbarians to go into this passage. The Romans therefore passed through it without encountering opposition, and some of them, arriving at the Gothic camp near by, for a short time tried to take it, but were unable to do so because of the strength of the stockade, although not many barbarians had been left behind in it. For the trench had been dug to an extraordinary depth, and since the earth taken from it had invariably been placed along its inner side, this reached a great height and so served as a wall[155]; and it was abundantly supplied with stakes, which were very sharp and close together, thus making a palisade. These defences so emboldened the barbarians that they began to repel the enemy vigorously. But one of the guards of Belisarius, Aquilinus by name, an exceedingly active man, seized a horse by the bridle and, bestriding it, leaped from the trench into the middle of the camp, where he slew some of the enemy. And when his opponents gathered about him and hurled great numbers of missiles, the horse was wounded and fell, but he himself unexpectedly made his escape through the midst of the enemy. So he went on foot with his companions toward the Pincian Gate. And overtaking the barbarians, who were still engaged in pursuing Roman horsemen,[156] they began to shoot at them from behind and killed some of them.

[335]Now when Trajan and his men perceived this, since they had meanwhile been reinforced by the horsemen who had been standing near by in readiness, they charged at full speed against their pursuers. Then at length the Goths, being now outgeneraled and unexpectedly caught between the forces of their enemy, began to be killed indiscriminately. And there was great slaughter of them, and very few escaped to their camps, and that with difficulty; meanwhile the others, fearing for the safety of all their strongholds, shut themselves in and remained in them thereafter, thinking that the Romans would come against them without the least delay. In this action one of the barbarians shot Trajan in the face, above the right eye and not far from the nose. And the whole of the iron point, penetrated the head and disappeared entirely, although the barb on it was large and exceedingly long, but the remainder of the arrow immediately fell to the ground without the application of force by anyone, in my opinion because the iron point had never been securely fastened to the shaft. Trajan, however, paid no heed to this at all, but continued none the less killing and pursuing the enemy. But in the fifth year afterward the tip of the iron of its own accord began to project visibly from his face. And this is now the third year since it has been slowly but steadily coming out. It is to be expected, therefore, that the whole barb will eventually come out, though not for a long time. But it has not been an impediment to the man in any way. So much then for these matters.[337]

FOOTNOTES:

[153] The regular harbour, Portus, was held by the Goths.

[154] Book V. xix. 6.

[155] Cf. Book V. xix. 11.

[156] These were the forces of Trajan and Diogenes.

VI

Now the barbarians straightway began to despair of winning the war and were considering how they might withdraw from Rome, inasmuch as they had suffered the ravages both of the pestilence and of the enemy, and were now reduced from many tens of thousands to a few men; and, not least of all, they were in a state of distress by reason of the famine, and while in name they were carrying on a siege, they were in fact being besieged by their opponents and were shut off from all necessities. And when they learned that still another army had come to their enemy from Byzantium both by land and by sea—not being informed as to its actual size, but supposing it to be as large as the free play of rumour was able to make it,—they became terrified at the danger and began to plan for their departure. They accordingly sent three envoys to Rome, one of whom was a Roman of note among the Goths, and he, coming before Belisarius, spoke as follows:

"That the war has not turned out to the advantage of either side each of us knows well, since we both have had actual experience of its hardships. For why should anyone in either army deny facts of which neither now remains in ignorance. And no one, I think, could deny, at least no one who does not lack understanding, that it is only senseless men who choose to go on suffering indefinitely merely to satisfy the contentious spirit which moves them for the moment, and refuse to find a solution of the troubles which harass them. And whenever this situation arises, it [339]is the duty of the commanders on both sides not to sacrifice the lives of their subjects to their own glory, but to choose the course which is just and expedient, not for themselves alone, but also for their opponents, and thus to put an end to present hardships. For moderation in one's demands affords a way out of all difficulties, but it is the very nature of contentiousness that it cannot accomplish any of the objects which are essential. Now we, on our part, have deliberated concerning the conclusion of this war and have come before you with proposals which are of advantage to both sides, wherein we waive, as we think, some portion even of our rights. And see to it that you likewise in your deliberations do not yield to a spirit of contentiousness respecting us and thus destroy yourselves as well as us, in preference to choosing the course which will be of advantage to yourselves. And it is fitting that both sides should state their case, not in continuous speech, but each interrupting the other on the spur of the moment, if anything that is said shall seem inappropriate. For in this way each side will be able to say briefly whatever it is minded to say, and at the same time the essential things will be accomplished." Belisarius replied: "There will be nothing to prevent the debate from proceeding in the manner you suggest, only let the words spoken by you be words of peace and of justice."

So the ambassadors of the Goths in their turn said: "You have done us an injustice, O Romans, in taking up arms wrongfully against us, your friends and allies. And what we shall say is, we think, well known to each one of you as well as to ourselves.[341] For the Goths did not obtain the land of Italy by wresting it from the Romans by force, but Odoacer in former times dethroned the emperor, changed the government of Italy to a tyranny, and so held it.[157] And Zeno, who then held the power of the East, though he wished to avenge his partner in the imperial office and to free this land from the usurper, was unable to destroy the authority of Odoacer. Accordingly he persuaded Theoderic, our ruler, although he was on the point of besieging him and Byzantium, not only to put an end to his hostility towards himself, in recollection of the honour which Theoderic had already received at his hands in having been made a patrician and consul of the Romans,[158] but also to punish Odoacer for his unjust treatment of Augustulus, and thereafter, in company with the Goths, to hold sway over the land as its legitimate and rightful rulers. It was in this way, therefore, that we took over the dominion of Italy, and we have preserved both the laws and the form of government as strictly as any who have ever been Roman emperors, and there is absolutely no law, either written or unwritten, introduced by Theoderic or by any of his successors on the throne of the Goths. And we have so scrupulously guarded for the Romans their practices pertaining to the worship of God and faith in Him, that not one of the Italians has changed his belief, either willingly or unwillingly, up to the present day, and when Goths have changed,[159] we have taken no notice of the matter. And indeed the sanctuaries of the Romans have received from us the highest honour; for no one who has taken refuge [343]in any of them has ever been treated with violence by any man; nay, more, the Romans themselves have continued to hold all the offices of the state, and not a single Goth has had a share in them. Let someone come forward and refute us, if he thinks that this statement of ours is not true. And one might add that the Goths have conceded that the dignity of the consulship should be conferred upon Romans each year by the emperor of the East. Such has been the course followed by us; but you, on your side, did not take the part of Italy while it was suffering at the hands of the barbarians and Odoacer, although it was not for a short time, but for ten years, that he treated the land outrageously; but now you do violence to us who have acquired it legitimately, though you have no business here. Do you therefore depart hence out of our way, keeping both that which is your own and whatever you have gained by plunder."

And Belisarius said: "Although your promise gave us to understand that your words would be brief and temperate, yet your discourse has been both long and not far from fraudulent in its pretensions. For Theoderic was sent by the Emperor Zeno in order to make war on Odoacer, not in order to hold the dominion of Italy for himself. For why should the emperor have been concerned to exchange one tyrant for another? But he sent him in order that Italy might be free and obedient to the emperor. And though Theoderic disposed of the tyrant in a satisfactory manner, in everything else he shewed an extraordinary lack of proper feeling; for he never thought of restoring the land to its rightful owner. But I, for my part, think that he who robs [345]another by violence and he who of his own will does not restore his neighbour's goods are equal. Now, as for me, I shall never surrender the emperor's country to any other. But if there is anything you wish to receive in place of it, I give you leave to speak."

And the barbarians said: "That everything which we have said is true no one of you can be unaware. But in order that we may not seem to be contentious, we give up to you Sicily, great as it is and of such wealth, seeing that without it you cannot possess Libya in security."

And Belisarius replied: "And we on our side permit the Goths to have the whole of Britain, which is much larger than Sicily and was subject to the Romans in early times. For it is only fair to make an equal return to those who first do a good deed or perform a kindness."

The barbarians: "Well, then, if we should make you a proposal concerning Campania also, or about Naples itself, will you listen to it?"

Belisarius: "No, for we are not empowered to administer the emperor's affairs in a way which is not in accord with his wish."

The barbarians: "Not even if we impose upon ourselves the payment of a fixed sum of money every year?"

Belisarius: "No, indeed. For we are not empowered to do anything else than guard the land for its owner."

The barbarians: "Come now, we must send [347]envoys to the emperor and make with him our treaty concerning the whole matter. And a definite time must also be appointed during which the armies will be bound to observe an armistice."

Belisarius: "Very well; let this be done. For never shall I stand in your way when you are making plans for peace."

After saying these things they each left the conference, and the envoys of the Goths withdrew to their own camp. And during the ensuing days they visited each other frequently and made the arrangements for the armistice, and they agreed that each side should put into the hands of the other some of its notable men as hostages to ensure the keeping of the armistice.

FOOTNOTES:

[157] 476 A.D. Cf. Book V. i. 6-8 and note.

[158] Cf. Book V. i. 10, 11.

[159] The Goths were Christians, but followed the Arian heresy.

VII

But while these negotiations were in progress at Rome, meanwhile the fleet of the Isaurians put in at the harbour[160] of the Romans and John with his men came to Ostia, and not one of the enemy hindered them either while bringing their ships to land or while making their camp. But in order that they might be able to pass the night safe from a sudden attack by the enemy, the Isaurians dug a deep trench close to the harbour and kept a constant guard by shifts of men, while John's soldiers made a barricade of their waggons about the camp and remained quiet. And when night came on Belisarius went to Ostia with a hundred horsemen, and after telling what had taken place in the engagement [349]and the agreement which had been made between the Romans and the Goths and otherwise encouraging them, he bade them bring their cargoes and come with all zeal to Rome. "For," he said, "I shall take care that the journey is free from danger." So he himself at early dawn rode back to the city, and Antonina together with the commanders began at daybreak to consider means of transporting the cargoes. But it seemed to them that the task was a hard one and beset with the greatest difficulties. For the oxen could hold out no longer, but all lay half-dead, and, furthermore, it was dangerous to travel over a rather narrow road with the waggons, and impossible to tow the barges on the river, as had formerly been the custom. For the road which is on the left[161] of the river was held by the enemy, as stated by me in the previous narrative,[162] and not available for the use of the Romans at that time, while the road on the other side of it is altogether unused, at least that part of it which follows the river-bank. They therefore selected the small boats belonging to the larger ships, put a fence of high planks around them on all sides, in order that the men on board might not be exposed to the enemy's shots, and embarked archers and sailors on them in numbers suitable for each boat. And after they had loaded the boats with all the freight they could carry, they waited for a favouring wind and set sail toward Rome by the Tiber, and a portion of the army followed them along the right[161] bank of the river to support them. But they left a [351]large number of Isaurians to guard the ships. Now where the course of the river was straight, they found no trouble in sailing, simply raising the sails of the boats; but where the stream wound about and took a course athwart the wind, and the sails received no impulse from it, the sailors had no slight toil in rowing and forcing the boats against the current. As for the barbarians, they sat in their camps and had no wish to hinder their enemy, either because they were terrified at the danger, or because they thought that the Romans would never by such means succeed in bringing in any provisions, and considered it contrary to their own interest, when a matter of no consequence was involved, to frustrate their hope of the armistice which Belisarius had already promised. Moreover, the Goths who were in Portus, though they could see their enemy constantly sailing by almost near enough to touch, made no move against them, but sat there wondering in amazement at the plan they had hit upon. And when the Romans had made the voyage up the river many times in the same way, and had thus conveyed all the cargoes into the city without interference, the sailors took the ships and withdrew with all speed, for it was already about the time of the winter solstice; and the rest of the army entered Rome, except, indeed, that Paulus remained in Ostia with some of the Isaurians.

And afterwards they gave hostages to one another to secure the keeping of the armistice, the Romans giving Zeno, and the Goths Ulias, a man of no mean station, with the understanding that during three months they should make no attack upon one [353]another, until the envoys should return from Byzantium and report the will of the emperor. And even if the one side or the other should initiate offences against their opponents, the envoys were nevertheless to be returned to their own nation. So the envoys of the barbarians went to Byzantium escorted by Romans, and Ildiger, the son-in-law of Antonina, came to Rome from Libya with not a few horsemen. And the Goths who were holding the stronghold at Portus abandoned the place by the order of Vittigis because their supplies were exhausted, and came to the camp in obedience to his summons. Whereupon Paulus with his Isaurians came from Ostia and took possession of it and held it. Now the chief reason why these barbarians were without provisions was that the Romans commanded the sea and did not allow any of the necessary supplies to be brought in to them. And it was for this reason that they also abandoned at about the same time a sea-coast city of great importance, Centumcellae[163] by name, that is, because they were short of provisions. This city is large and populous, lying to the west of Rome, in Tuscany, distant from it about two hundred and eighty stades. And after taking possession of it the Romans went on and extended their power still more, for they took also the town of Albani, which lies to the east of Rome, the enemy having evacuated it at that time for the same reason, and they had already surrounded the barbarians on all sides and now held them between their forces. The Goths, therefore, were in a mood to break the agreement and do some harm to the Romans. So they sent envoys to Belisarius [355]and asserted that they had been unjustly treated during a truce; for when Vittigis had summoned the Goths who were in Portus to perform some service for him, Paulus and the Isaurians had seized and taken possession of the fort there for no good reason. And they made this same false charge regarding Albani and Centumcellae, and threatened that, unless he should give these places back to them, they would resent it. But Belisarius laughed and sent them away, saying that this charge was but a pretext, and that no one was ignorant of the reason why the Goths had abandoned these places. And thereafter the two sides were somewhat suspicious of one another.

But later, when Belisarius saw that Rome was abundantly supplied with soldiers, he sent many horsemen to places far distant from Rome, and commanded John, the nephew of Vitalian, and the horsemen under his command, eight hundred in number, to pass the winter near the city of Alba, which lies in Picenum; and with him he sent four hundred of the men of Valerian, whom Damianus, the nephew of Valerian, commanded, and eight hundred men of his own guards who were especially able warriors. And in command of these he put two spearmen, Suntas and Adegis, and ordered them to follow John wherever he should lead; and he gave John instructions that as long as he saw the enemy was keeping the agreement made between them, he should remain quiet; but whenever he found that the armistice had been violated by them, he should do as follows: With his whole force he was to make a sudden raid and overrun the land of Picenum, visiting all the districts of that region and reaching [357]each one before the report of his coming. For in this whole land there was virtually not a single man left, since all, as it appeared, had marched against Rome, but everywhere there were women and children of the enemy and money. He was instructed, therefore, to enslave or plunder whatever he found, taking care never to injure any of the Romans living there. And if he should happen upon any place which had men and defences, as he probably would, he was to make an attempt upon it with his whole force. And if he was able to capture it, he was to go forward, but if it should so happen that his attempt was unsuccessful, he was to march back or remain there. For if he should go forward and leave such a fortress in his rear, he would be involved in the greatest danger, since his men would never be able to defend themselves easily, if they should be harassed by their opponents. He was also to keep the whole booty intact, in order that it might be divided fairly and properly among the army. Then with a laugh he added this also: "For it is not fair that the drones should be destroyed with great labour by one force, while others, without having endured any hardship at all, enjoy the honey." So after giving these instructions, Belisarius sent John with his army.

And at about the same time Datius, the priest of Milan, and some notable men among the citizens came to Rome and begged Belisarius to send them a few guards. For they declared that they were themselves able without any trouble to detach from [359]the Goths not only Milan, but the whole of Liguria also, and to recover them for the emperor. Now this city is situated in Liguria, and lies about half way between the city of Ravenna and the Alps on the borders of Gaul; for from either one it is a journey of eight days to Milan for an unencumbered traveller; and it is the first of the cities of the West, after Rome at least, both in size and in population and in general prosperity. And Belisarius promised to fulfil their request, but detained them there during the winter season.

FOOTNOTES:

[160] Ostia, since the regular harbour, Portus, was held by the Goths.

[161] *i.e.* facing upstream.

[162] Book IV. xxvi. 14.

[163] Modern Civita Vecchia.

VIII

Such was the course of these events. But the envy of fortune was already swelling against the Romans, when she saw their affairs progressing successfully and well, and wishing to mingle some evil with this good, she inspired a quarrel, on a trifling pretext, between Belisarius and Constantinus; and how this grew and to what end it came I shall now go on to relate. There was a certain Presidius, a Roman living at Ravenna, and a man of no mean station. This Presidius had given offence to the Goths at the time when Vittigis was about to march against Rome, and so he set out with some few of his domestics ostensibly on a hunting expedition, and went into exile; he had communicated his plan to no one and took none of his property with him, except indeed that he himself carried two daggers, the scabbards of which happened to be adorned with much gold and [361]precious stones. And when he came to Spolitium, he lodged in a certain temple outside the fortifications. And when Constantinus, who happened to be still tarrying there,[164] heard of this, he sent one of his guards, Maxentiolus, and took away from him both the daggers for no good reason. The man was deeply offended by what had taken place, and set out for Rome with all speed and came to Belisarius, and Constantinus also arrived there not long afterward; for the Gothic army was already reported to be not far away. Now as long as the affairs of the Romans were critical and in confusion, Presidius remained silent; but when he saw that the Romans were gaining the upper hand and that the envoys of the Goths had been sent to the emperor, as has been told by me above, he frequently approached Belisarius reporting the injustice and demanding that he assist him in obtaining his rights. And Belisarius reproached Constantinus many times himself, and many times through others, urging him to clear himself of the guilt of an unjust deed and of a dishonouring report. But Constantinus—for it must needs be that evil befall him—always lightly evaded the charge and taunted the wronged man. But on one occasion Presidius met Belisarius riding on horseback in the forum, and he laid hold of the horse's bridle, and crying out with a loud voice asked whether the laws of the emperor said that, whenever anyone fleeing from the barbarians comes to them as a suppliant, they should rob him by violence of whatever he may chance to have in his hands. And though many men gathered about and commanded him with threats to [363]let go his hold of the bridle, he did not let go until at last Belisarius promised to give him the daggers. On the following day, therefore, Belisarius called Constantinus and many of the commanders to an apartment in the palace, and after going over what had happened on the previous day urged him even at that late time to restore the daggers. But Constantinus refused to do so; nay, he would more gladly throw them into the waters of the Tiber than give them to Presidius. And Belisarius, being by now mastered by anger, enquired whether Constantinus did not think that he was subject to his orders. And he agreed to obey him in all other things, for this was the emperor's will; this command, however, which at the present time he was laying upon him, he would never obey. Belisarius then commanded his guards to enter, whereupon Constantinus said: "In order, plainly, to have them kill me." "By no means," said Belisarius, "but to have them compel your bodyguard Maxentiolus, who forcibly carried away the daggers for you, to restore to the man what he took from him by violence." But Constantinus, thinking that he was to die that very instant, wished to do some great deed before he should suffer anything himself. He accordingly drew the dagger which hung by his thigh and suddenly thrust it at the belly of Belisarius. And he in consternation stepped back, and by throwing his arms around Bessas, who was standing near, succeeded in escaping the blow. Then Constantinus, still boiling with anger, made after him; but Ildiger and Valerian, seeing what was [365]being done, laid hold of his hands, one of the right and the other of the left, and dragged him back. And at this point the guards entered whom Belisarius had summoned a moment before, snatched the dagger of Constantinus from his hand with great violence, and seized him amid a great uproar. At the moment they did him no harm, out of respect, I suppose, to the officers present, but led him away to another room at the command of Belisarius, and at a somewhat later time put him to death. This was the only unholy deed done by

Belisarius, and it was in no way worthy of the character of the man; for he always shewed great gentleness in his treatment of all others. But it had to be, as I have said, that evil should befall Constantinus.

FOOTNOTE:

[164] Cf. Book V. xvi. 1 ff.

IX

And the Goths not long after this wished to strike a blow at the fortifications of Rome. And first they sent some men by night into one of the aqueducts, from which they themselves had taken out the water at the beginning of this war.[165] And with lamps and torches in their hands they explored the entrance into the city by this way. Now it happened that not far from the small Pincian Gate an arch of this aqueduct[166] had a sort of crevice in it, and one of the guards saw the light through this and told his companions; but they said that he had seen a wolf passing by his post. For at that point it so happened that the structure of the aqueduct did not rise high above the ground, and they thought that the guard had imagined the wolf's eyes to be fire. So [367]those barbarians who explored the aqueduct, upon reaching the middle of the city, where there was an upward passage built in olden times leading to the palace itself, came upon some masonry there which allowed them neither to advance beyond that point nor to use the ascent at all. This masonry had been put in by Belisarius as an act of precaution at the beginning of this siege, as has been set forth by me in the preceding narrative.[167] So they decided first to remove one small stone from the wall and then to go back immediately, and when they returned to Vittigis, they displayed the stone and reported the whole situation. And while he was considering his scheme with the best of the Goths, the Romans who were on guard at the Pincian Gate recalled among themselves on the following day the suspicion of the wolf. But when the story was passed around and came to Belisarius, the general did not treat the matter carelessly, but immediately sent some of the notable men in the army, together with the guardsman Diogenes, down into the aqueduct and bade them investigate everything with all speed. And they found all along the aqueduct the lamps of the enemy and the ashes which had dropped from their torches, and after observing the masonry where the stone had been taken out by the Goths, they reported to Belisarius. For this reason he personally kept the aqueduct under close guard; and the Goths, perceiving it, desisted from this attempt.

But later on the barbarians went so far as to plan an open attack against the fortifications. So they waited for the time of lunch, and bringing up ladders [369]and fire, when their enemy were least expecting them, made an assault upon the small Pincian Gate, emboldened by the hope of capturing the city by a sudden attack, since not many soldiers had been left there. But it happened that Ildiger and his men were keeping guard at that time; for all were assigned by turns to guard-duty. So when he saw the enemy advancing in disorder, he went out against them before they were yet drawn up in line of battle and while they were advancing in great disarray, and routing those who were opposite him without any trouble he slew many. And a great outcry and commotion arose throughout the city, as was to be expected, and the Romans gathered as quickly as possible to all parts of the fortifications; whereupon the barbarians after a short time retired to their camp baffled.

But Vittigis resorted again to a plot against the wall. Now there was a certain part of it that was especially vulnerable, where the bank of the Tiber is, because at this place the Romans of old, confident in the protection afforded by the stream, had built the wall carelessly, making it low and altogether without towers; Vittigis therefore hoped to capture the city rather easily from that quarter. For indeed there was not even any garrison there of any consequence, as it happened. He therefore bribed with money two Romans who lived near the church of Peter the Apostle to pass along by the guards there at about nightfall carrying a skin full of wine, and in some way or other, by making a show of friendship, to give it to them, and then to sit drinking with them well on into the night; and they were to throw [371]into the cup of each guard a sleep-producing drug which Vittigis had given them. And he stealthily got ready some skiffs, which he kept at the other bank; as soon as the guards should be overcome by sleep, some of the barbarians, acting in concert, were to cross the river in these, taking ladders with them, and make the assault on the wall. And he made ready the entire army with the intention of capturing the whole city by storm. After these arrangements were all complete, one of the two men who had been prepared by Vittigis for this service (for it was not fated that Rome should be captured by this army of the Goths) came of his own accord to Belisarius and revealed everything, and told who the other man was. So this man under torture brought to light all that he was about to do and displayed the drug which Vittigis had given him. And Belisarius first mutilated his nose and ears and then sent him riding on an ass into the enemy's camp. And when the barbarians saw him, they realised that God would not allow their purposes to have free course, and that therefore the city could never be captured by them.

FOOTNOTES:

[165] Book V. xix. 13.

[166] The *Aqua Virgo*.

[167] Book V. xix. 18.

X

But while these things were happening, Belisarius wrote to John and commanded him to begin operations. And he with his two thousand horsemen began to go about the land of Picenum and to [373]plunder everything before him, treating the women and children of the enemy as slaves. And when Ulitheus, the uncle of Vittigis, confronted him with an army of Goths, he defeated them in battle and killed Ulitheus himself and almost the whole army of the enemy. For this reason no one dared any longer to engage with him. But when he came to the city of Auximus,[168] though he learned that it contained a Gothic garrison of inconsiderable size, yet in other respects he observed that the place was strong and impossible to capture. And for this reason he was quite unwilling to lay siege to it, but departing from there as quickly as he could, he moved forward. And he did this same thing at the city of Urbinus,[169] but at Ariminum,[170] which is one day's journey distant from Ravenna, he marched into the city at the invitation of the Romans. Now all the barbarians who were keeping guard there were very suspicious of the Roman inhabitants, and as soon as they learned that this army was approaching, they withdrew and ran until they reached Ravenna. And thus John secured Ariminum; but he had meanwhile left in his rear a garrison of the enemy both at Auximus and at Urbinus, not because he had forgotten the commands of Belisarius, nor because he was carried away by unreasoning boldness, since he had wisdom as well as energy, but because he reasoned—correctly, as it turned out—that if the Goths learned that the Roman army was close to Ravenna, they would instantly break up the siege of Rome because of their fears regarding this place. And in fact his reasoning proved to be true. For as [375]soon as Vittigis and the army of the Goths heard that Ariminum was held by him, they were plunged into great fear regarding Ravenna, and abandoning all other considerations, they straightway made their withdrawal, as will be told by me directly. And John won great fame from this deed, though he was renowned even before. For he was a daring and efficient man in the highest degree, unflinching before danger, and in his daily life shewing at all times a certain austerity and ability to endure hardship unsurpassed by any barbarian or common soldier. Such a man was John. And Matasuntha, the wife of Vittigis, who was exceedingly hostile to her husband because he had taken her to wife by violence in the beginning,[171] upon learning that John had come to Ariminum was absolutely overcome by joy, and sending a messenger to him opened secret negotiations with him concerning marriage and the betrayal of the city.

So these two kept sending messengers to each other without the knowledge of the rest and arranging these matters. But when the Goths learned what had happened at Ariminum, and when at the same time all their provisions had failed them, and the three months' time had already expired, they began to make their withdrawal, although they had not as yet received any information as far as the envoys were concerned. Now it was about the spring equinox, and one year had been spent in the siege and nine days in addition, when the Goths, having burned all their camps, set out at daybreak. And the Romans, seeing their opponents in flight, were at a loss how to deal with the situation. For it [377]so happened that the majority of the horsemen were not present at that time, since they had been sent to various places, as has been stated by me above,[172] and they did not think that by themselves they were a match for so great a multitude of the enemy. However, Belisarius armed all the infantry and cavalry. And when he saw that more than half of the enemy had crossed the bridge, he led the army out through the small Pincian Gate, and the hand-to-hand battle which ensued proved to be equal to any that had preceded it. At the beginning the barbarians withstood their enemy vigorously, and many on both sides fell in the first encounter; but afterwards the Goths turned to flight and brought upon themselves a great and overwhelming calamity; for each man for himself was rushing to cross the bridge first. As a result of this they became very much crowded and suffered most cruelly, for they were being killed both by each other and by the enemy. Many, too, fell off the bridge on either side into the Tiber, sank with all their arms, and perished. Finally, after losing in this way the most of their number, the remainder joined those who had crossed before. And Longinus the Isaurian and Mundilas, the guards of Belisarius, made themselves conspicuous for their valour in this battle. But while Mundilas, after engaging with four barbarians in turn and killing them all, was himself saved, Longinus, having proved himself the chief cause of the rout of the enemy, fell where he fought, leaving the Roman army great regret for his loss. [379]

FOOTNOTES:

[168] Modern Osimo.

[169] Modern Urbino.

[170] Modern Rimini.

[171] Cf. Book V. xi. 27.

[172] Chap. vii. 25.

XI

Now Vittigis with the remainder of his army marched toward Ravenna; and he strengthened the fortified places with a great number of guards, leaving in Clusium,[173] the city of Tuscany, one thousand men and Gibimer as commander, and in Urviventus[174] an equal number, over whom he set Albilas, a Goth, as commander. And he left Uligisalus in Tudera[175] with four hundred men. And in the land of Picenum he left in the fortress of Petra four hundred men who had lived there previously, and in Auximus, which is the largest of all the cities of that country, he left four thousand Goths selected for their valour and a very energetic commander, Visandus by name, and two thousand men with Moras in the city of Urbinus. There are also two other fortresses, Caesena and Monteferetra,[176] in each of which he established a garrison of not less than five hundred men. Then he himself with the rest of the army moved straight for Ariminum with the purpose of laying siege to it.

But it happened that Belisarius, as soon as the Goths had broken up the siege of Rome, had sent Ildiger and Martinus with a thousand horsemen, in order that by travelling more quickly by another road they might arrive at Ariminum first, and he directed them promptly to remove John from the city and all those with him, and to put in their place fully enough men to guard the city, taking them [381]from the fortress which is on the Ionian Gulf, Ancon by name, two days' journey distant from Ariminum. For he had already taken possession of it not long before, having sent Conon with no small force of Isaurians and Thracians. It was his hope that if unsupported infantry under commanders of no great note should hold Ariminum, the Gothic forces would never undertake its siege, but would regard it with contempt and so go at once to Ravenna, and that if they should decide to besiege Ariminum, the provisions there would suffice for the infantry for a somewhat longer time; and he thought also that two thousand horsemen,[177] attacking from outside with the rest of the army, would in all probability do the enemy great harm and drive them more easily to abandon the siege. It was with this purpose that

Belisarius gave such orders to Martinus and Ildiger and their men. And they, by travelling over the Flaminian Way, arrived long before the barbarians. For since the Goths were moving in a great throng, they proceeded in a more leisurely manner, and they were compelled to make certain long detours, both because of the lack of provisions, and because they preferred not to pass close to the fortresses on the Flaminian Way, Narnia and Spolitium and Perusia, since these were in the hands of the enemy, as has been stated above.[178]

When the Roman army arrived at Petra, they made an attack upon the fortress there, regarding it as an incident of their expedition. Now this fortress was not devised by man, but it was made by the nature of [383]the place; for the road passes through an extremely mountainous country at that place. On the right of this road a river descends which no man can ford because of the swiftness of the current, and on the left not far away rises a sheer rock which reaches to such a height that men who might chance to be standing on its summit, as seen by those below, resemble in size the smallest birds. And in olden times there was no passage through as one went forward. For the end of the rock reaches to the very stream of the river, affording no room for those who travel that way to pass by. So the men of ancient times constructed a tunnel at that point, and made there a gate for the place.[179] And they also closed up the greatest part of the other[180] entrance, leaving only enough space for a small gate there also, and thus rendered the place a natural fortress, which they call by the fitting name of Petra. So the men of Martinus and Ildiger first made an attack upon one of the two gates,[181] and shot many missiles, but they accomplished nothing, although the barbarians there made no defence at all; but afterwards they forced their way up the cliff behind the fortress and hurled stones from there upon the heads of the Goths. And they, hurriedly and in great confusion, entered their houses and remained quiet. And then the Romans, unable to hit any of the enemy with the stones they threw, devised the following plan. They broke off large pieces from the cliff and, many of them pushing together, hurled them down, aiming at the houses. And wherever these in their fall did no more than just graze the building, [385]they yet gave the whole fortress a considerable shock and reduced the barbarians to great fear. Consequently the Goths stretched out their hands to those who were still about the gate and surrendered themselves and the fort, with the condition that they themselves should remain free from harm, being slaves of the emperor and subject to Belisarius. And Ildiger and Martinus removed the most of them and led them away, putting them on a basis of complete equality with themselves, but some few they left there, together with their wives and children. And they also left something of a garrison of Romans. Thence they proceeded to Ancon, and taking with them many of the infantry in that place on the third day reached Ariminum, and announced the will of Belisarius. But John was not only unwilling himself to follow them, but also proposed to retain Damianus with the four hundred.[182] So they left there the infantry and retired thence with all speed, taking the spearmen and guards of Belisarius.

FOOTNOTES:

[173] Modern Chiusi.

[174] Urbs Vetus, modern Orvieto.

[175] Tuder or Tudertum, modern Todi.

[176] Modern Montefeltro.

[177] i.e. the force which John had when he had set out on his raid of Picenum (cf. Chap. x. 1) and with which he was now holding Ariminum.

[178] Book V. xxix. 3.

[179] The tunnel was made by the Emperor Vespasian, 76 A.D. This gate was at the southern end.

[180] i.e. northern.

[181] The upper, or southern, gate.

[182] Cf. Chap. vii. 26.

XII

And not long afterward Vittigis and his whole army arrived at Ariminum, where they established their camp and began the siege. And they immediately constructed a wooden tower higher than the circuit-wall of the city and resting on four wheels, and drew it toward that part of the wall which seemed to them most vulnerable. But in order that they might not have the same experience here which they had before the fortifications of Rome, they did not use oxen to draw the tower, but hid themselves within it and thus [387]hauled it forward. And there was a stairway of great breadth inside the tower on which the barbarians in great numbers were to make the ascent easily, for they hoped that as soon as they should place the tower against the fortifications, they would have no trouble in stepping thence to the parapet of the wall; for they had made the tower high with this in view. So when they had come close to the fortifications with this engine of war, they remained quiet for the time, since it was already growing dark, and stationing guards about the tower they all went off to pass the night, supposing that they would meet with no obstacle whatever. And indeed there was nothing in their way, not even a trench between them and the wall, except an exceedingly small one.

As for the Romans, they passed the night in great fear, supposing that on the morrow they would perish. But John, neither yielding to despair in face of the danger nor being greatly agitated by fear, devised the following plan. Leaving the others on guard at their posts, he himself took the Isaurians, who carried pickaxes and various other tools of this kind, and went outside the fortifications; it was late in the night and no word had been given beforehand to anyone in the city; and once outside the wall, he commanded his men in silence to dig the trench deeper. So they did as directed, and as they dug they kept putting the earth which they took out of the trench upon the side of it nearer the city-wall, and there it served them as an earthwork. And since they were unobserved for a long time by the enemy, who were sleeping, [389]they soon made the trench both deep and sufficiently wide, at the place where the fortifications were especially vulnerable and where the barbarians were going to make the assault with their engine of war. But far on in the night the enemy, perceiving what was being done, charged at full speed against those who were digging, and John went inside the fortifications with the Isaurians, since the trench was now in a most satisfactory condition.

But at daybreak Vittigis noted what had been accomplished and in his exceeding vexation at the occurrence executed some of the guards; however, he was as eager as before to bring his engine to bear, and so commanded the Goths to throw a great number of faggots as quickly as possible into the trench, and then by drawing the tower over them to bring it into position. This they proceeded to do as Vittigis commanded, with all zeal, although their opponents kept fighting them back from the wall with the utmost vigour. But when the weight of the tower came upon the faggots they naturally yielded and sank down. For this reason the barbarians were quite unable to go forward with the engine, because the ground became still more steep before them, where the Romans had heaped up the earth as I have stated. Fearing, therefore, that when night came on the enemy would sally forth and set fire to the engine, they began to draw it back again. This was precisely what John was eager to prevent with all his power, and so he armed his soldiers, called them all together, and exhorted them as follows:[391]

"My men, who share this danger common to us all, if it would please any man among you to live and see those whom he has left at home, let him realize that the only hope he has of obtaining these things lies in nothing but his own hands. For when Belisarius sent us forth in the beginning, hope and desire for many things made us eager for the task. For we never suspected that we should be besieged in the country along the coast, since the Romans command the sea so completely, nor would one have supposed that the emperor's army would so far neglect us. But apart from these considerations, at that time we were prompted to boldness by an opportunity to display our loyalty to the state and by the glory which we should acquire in the sight of all men as the result of our struggles. But as things now stand, we cannot possibly survive save by courage, and we are obliged to undergo this danger with no other end in view than the saving of our own lives. Therefore, if any of you perchance lay claim to valour, all such have the opportunity to prove themselves brave men, if any men in the world have, and thereby to cover themselves with glory. For they achieve a fair name, not who overpower those weaker than themselves, but who, though inferior in equipment, still win the victory by the greatness of their souls. And as for those in whom the love of life has been more deeply implanted, it will be of advantage to these especially to be bold, for it is true of all men, as a general thing, that when their fortunes stand on the razor's edge, as is now the case with us, they may be saved only by scorning the danger."

With these words John led his army out against the enemy, leaving some few men to guard the [393]battlement. But the enemy withstood them bravely, and the battle became exceedingly fierce. And with great difficulty and late in the day the barbarians succeeded in bringing the tower back to their own camp. However, they lost so great a number of their fighting men that they decided thenceforth to make no further attacks upon the wall, but in despair of succeeding that way, they remained quiet, expecting that their enemy would yield to them under stress of famine. For all their provisions had already failed them completely, since they had not found any place from which they could bring in a sufficient supply.

Such was the course of events here. But as for Belisarius, he sent to the representatives of Milan[183] a thousand men, Isaurians and Thracians. The Isaurians were commanded by Ennes, the Thracians by Paulus, while Mundilas was set over them all and commanded in person, having as his guard some few of the guardsmen of Belisarius. And with them was also Fidelius, who had been made praetorian prefect. For since he was a native of Milan, he was regarded as a suitable person to go with this army, having as he did some influence in Liguria. They set sail, accordingly, from the harbour of Rome and put in at Genoa, which is the last city in

Tuscany and well situated as a port of call for the voyage to Gaul and to Spain. There they left their ships and travelling by land moved forward, placing the boats of the ships on their waggons, in order that nothing might prevent their crossing the river Po. It was by this means, in any event, that they made the crossing of the river. And when they reached the city of Ticinum,[184] after crossing the Po, the Goths came out against them and [395]engaged them in battle. And they were not only numerous but also excellent troops, since all the barbarians who lived in that region had deposited the most valuable of their possessions in Ticinum, as being a place which had strong defences, and had left there a considerable garrison. So a fierce battle took place, but the Romans were victorious, and routing their opponents, they slew a great number and came within a little of capturing the city in the pursuit. For it was only with difficulty that the barbarians succeeded in shutting the gates, so closely did their enemy press upon their heels. And as the Romans were marching away, Fidelius went into a temple there to pray, and was the last to leave. But by some chance his horse stumbled and he fell. And since he had fallen very near the fortifications, the Goths seeing him came out and killed him without being observed by the enemy. Wherefore, when this was afterwards discovered by Mundilas and the Romans, they were greatly distressed.

Then, leaving Ticinum, they arrived at the city of Milan and secured this city with the rest of Liguria without a battle. When Vittigis learned about this, he sent a large army with all speed and Uraïas, his own nephew, as commander. And Theudibert, the leader of the Franks, sent him at his request ten thousand men as allies, not of the Franks themselves, but Burgundians, in order not to appear to be doing injury to the emperor's cause. For it was given out that the Burgundians made the expedition willingly and of their own choice, not as obeying the command of Theudibert. And the Goths, joined by these troops, came to Milan, made camp and began a siege [397]when the Romans were least expecting them. At any rate the Romans, through this action, found it impossible to bring in any kind of provisions, but they were immediately in distress for want of necessities. Indeed, even the guarding of the walls was not being maintained by the regular soldiers, for it so happened that Mundilas had occupied all the cities near Milan which had defences, namely Bergomum, Comum, and Novaria,[185] as well as some other strongholds, and in every place had established a considerable garrison, while he himself with about three hundred men remained in Milan, and with him Ennes and Paulus. Consequently and of necessity the inhabitants of the city were regularly keeping guard in turn. Such was the progress of events in Liguria, and the winter drew to its close, and the third year came to an end in this war, the history of which Procopius has written.

FOOTNOTES:

[183] Cf. Chap. vii. 35.

[184] Modern Pavia.

[185] Modern Bergamo, Como, and Novara.

XIII

And Belisarius at about the time of the summer solstice marched against Vittigis and the Gothic army, leaving a few men to act as a garrison in Rome, but taking all the others with him. And he sent some men to Tudera and Clusium, with orders to make fortified camps there, and he was intending to follow them and assist in besieging the barbarians at those places. But when the barbarians learned that the army was approaching, they did not wait to face the danger, but sent envoys to Belisarius, promising to surrender both themselves and the two cities, with the condition that they should remain free from harm. And when he came there, they fulfilled their [399]promise. And Belisarius removed all the Goths from these towns and sent them to Sicily and Naples, and after establishing a garrison in Clusium and in Tudera, he led his army forward.

But meanwhile Vittigis had sent another army, under command of Vacimus, to Auximus, commanding it to join forces with the Goths there, and with them to go against the enemy in Ancon and make an attempt upon that fortress. Now this Ancon is a sort of pointed rock, and indeed it is from this circumstance that it has taken its name; for it is exceedingly like an "elbow." And it is about eighty stades distant from the city of Auximus, whose port it is. And the defences of the fortress lie upon the pointed rock in a position of security, but all the buildings outside, though they are many, have been from ancient times unprotected by a wall. Now as soon as Conon, who was in command of the garrison of the place, heard that the forces of Vacimus were coming against him and were already not far away, he made an exhibition of thoughtless folly. For thinking it too small a thing to preserve free from harm merely the fortress and its inhabitants together with the soldiers, he left the fortifications entirely destitute of soldiers, and leading them all out to a distance of about five stades, arrayed them in line of battle, without, however, making the phalanx a deep one at all, but thin enough to surround the entire base of the mountain, as if for a hunt. But when these troops saw that the enemy were greatly superior to them in number, they turned their backs and straightway fled to the fortress. And the barbarians, following close upon them, slew on the spot [401]most of their number—those who did not succeed in getting inside the circuit-wall in time—and then placed ladders against the wall and attempted the ascent. Some also began burning the houses outside the fortress. And the Romans who resided habitually in the fortress, being terror-stricken at what was taking place, at first opened the small gate and received the soldiers as they fled in complete disorder. But when they saw the barbarians close at hand and pressing upon the fugitives, fearing that they would charge in with them, they closed the gates as quickly as they could, and letting down ropes from the battlement, saved a number by drawing them up, and among them Conon himself. But the barbarians scaled the wall by means of their ladders and came within a little of capturing the fortress by storm, and would have succeeded if two men had not made a display of remarkable deeds by valorously pushing off the battlements those who had already got upon the wall; one of these two was a bodyguard of Belisarius, a Thracian named Ulimuth, and the other a bodyguard of Valerian, named Gouboulgoudou, a Massagete by birth. These two men had happened by some chance to come by ship to Ancon a little before; and in this struggle, by warding off with their swords those who were scaling the wall, they saved the fortress contrary to expectation, but they themselves were carried from the battlement half dead, their whole bodies hacked with many wounds.

At that time it was reported to Belisarius that Narses had come with a great army from Byzantium and was in Picenum. Now this Narses[186] was a eunuch [403]and guardian of the royal treasures, but for the rest keen and more energetic than would be expected of a eunuch. And five thousand soldiers followed him, of whom the several detachments were commanded by different men, among whom were Justinus, the general of Illyricum, and another Narses, who had previously come to the land of the Romans as a deserter from the Armenians who are subject to the Persians; with him had come his brother Aratius,[187] who, as it happened, had joined

Belisarius a little before this with another army. And about two thousand of the Erulian nation also followed him, commanded by Visandus and Aluith and Phanitheus.

FOOTNOTES:

[186] He was an Armenian of Persia; see Book I. xv. 31.

[187] Book I. xv. 31.

XIV

Now as to who in the world the Eruli are, and how they entered into alliance with the Romans, I shall forthwith explain.[188] They used to dwell beyond the Ister[189] River from of old, worshipping a great host of gods, whom it seemed to them holy to appease even by human sacrifices. And they observed many customs which were not in accord with those of other men. For they were not permitted to live either when they grew old or when they fell sick, but as soon as one of them was overtaken by old age or by sickness, it became necessary for him to ask his relatives to remove him from the world as quickly as possible. And these relatives would pile up a quantity of wood to a great height and lay the man on top of the wood, and then they would send one of the Eruli, but not a relative of the man, to his side [405]with a dagger; for it was not lawful for a kinsman to be his slayer. And when the slayer of their relative had returned, they would straightway burn the whole pile of wood, beginning at the edges. And after the lire had ceased, they would immediately collect the bones and bury them in the earth. And when a man of the Eruli died, it was necessary for his wife, if she laid claim to virtue and wished to leave a fair name behind her, to die not long afterward beside the tomb of her husband by hanging herself with a rope. And if she did not do this, the result was that she was in ill repute thereafter and an offence to the relatives of her husband. Such were the customs observed by the Eruli in ancient times.

But as time went on they became superior to all the barbarians who dwelt about them both in power and in numbers, and, as was natural, they attacked and vanquished them severally and kept plundering their possessions by force. And finally they made the Lombards, who were Christians, together with several other nations, subject and tributary to themselves, though the barbarians of that region were not accustomed to that sort of thing; but the Eruli were led to take this course by love of money and a lawless spirit. 491 A.D. When, however, Anastasius took over the Roman empire, the Eruli, having no longer anyone in the world whom they could assail, laid down their arms and remained quiet, and they observed peace in this way for a space of three years. But the people themselves, being exceedingly vexed, began to abuse their leader Rodolphus without restraint, and going to him constantly they called him cowardly and effeminate, and railed at him in a [407]most unruly manner, taunting him with certain other names besides. And Rodolphus, being quite unable to bear the insult, marched against the Lombards, who were doing no wrong, without charging against them any fault or alleging any violation of their agreement, but bringing upon them a war which had no real cause. And when the Lombards got word of this, they sent to Rodolphus and made enquiry and demanded that he should state the charge on account of which the Eruli were coming against them in arms, agreeing that if they had deprived the Eruli of any of the tribute, then they would instantly pay it with large interest; and if their grievance was that only a moderate tribute had been imposed upon them, then the Lombards would never be reluctant to make it greater. Such were the offers which the envoys made, but Rodolphus with a threat sent them away and marched forward. And they again sent other envoys to him on the same mission and supplicated him with many entreaties. And when the second envoys had fared in the same way, a third embassy came to him and forbade the Eruli on any account to bring upon them a war without excuse. For if they should come against them with such a purpose, they too, not willingly, but under the direst necessity, would array themselves against their assailants, calling upon God as their witness, the slightest breath of whose favour, turning the scales, would be a match for all the strength of men; and He, in all likelihood, would be moved by the causes of the war and would determine the issue of the fight for both sides accordingly. So they spoke, thinking in this way to terrify their assailants, [409]but the Eruli, shrinking from nothing whatever, decided to meet the Lombards in battle. And when the two armies came close to one another, it so happened that the sky above the Lombards was obscured by a sort of cloud, black and very thick, but above the Eruli it was exceedingly clear. And judging by this one would have supposed that the Eruli were entering the conflict to their own harm; for there ran be no more forbidding portent than this for barbarians as they go into battle. However, the Eruli gave no heed even to this, but in absolute disregard of it they advanced against their enemy with utter contempt, estimating the outcome of war by mere superiority of numbers. But when the battle came to close quarters, many of the Eruli perished and Rodolphus himself also perished, and the rest fled at full speed, forgetting all their courage. And since their enemy followed them up, the most of them fell on the field of battle and only a few succeeded in saving themselves.

For this reason the Eruli were no longer able to tarry in their ancestral homes, but departing from there as quickly as possible they kept moving forward, traversing the whole country which is beyond the Ister River, together with their wives and children. But when they reached a land where the Rogi dwelt of old, a people who had joined the Gothic host and gone to Italy, they settled in that place. But since they were pressed by famine, because they were in a barren land, they removed from there not long afterward, and came to a place close to the country of the[411] Gepaedes.[190] And at first the Gepaedes permitted them to dwell there and be neighbours to them, since they came as suppliants. But afterwards for no good reason the Gepaedes began to practise unholy deeds upon them. For they violated their women and seized their cattle and other property, and abstained from no wickedness whatever, and finally began an unjust attack upon them. And the Eruli, unable to bear all this any longer, crossed the Ister River and decided to live as neighbours to the Romans in that region; this was during the reign of the Emperor Anastasius, who received them with great friendliness and allowed them to settle where they were. But a short time afterwards these barbarians gave him offence by their lawless treatment of the Romans there, and for this reason he sent an army against them. And the Romans, after defeating them in battle, slew most of their number, and had ample opportunity to destroy them all. But the remainder of them threw themselves upon the mercy of the generals and begged them to spare their lives and to have them as allies and servants of the emperor thereafter. And when Anastasius learned this, he was pleased, and consequently a number of the Eruli were left; however, they neither became allies of the Romans, nor did they do them any good.

---

527 A.D.

But when Justinian took over the empire, he bestowed upon them good lands and other possessions, and thus completely succeeded in winning their friendship and persuaded them all to become[413] Christians. As a result of this they adopted a gentler manner of life and decided to submit themselves wholly to the laws of the Christians, and in keeping with the terms of their alliance they are generally arrayed with the Romans against their enemies. They are still, however, faithless toward them, and since they are given to avarice, they are eager to do violence to their neighbours, feeling no shame at such conduct. And they mate in an unholy manner, especially men with asses, and they are the basest of all men and utterly abandoned rascals.

Afterwards, although some few of them remained at peace with the Romans, as will be told by me in the following narrative,[191] all the rest revolted for the following reason. The Eruli, displaying their beastly and fanatical character against their own "rex," one Ochus by name, suddenly killed the man for no good reason at all, laying against him no other charge than that they wished to be without a king thereafter. And yet even before this, while their king did have the title, he had practically no advantage over any private citizen whomsoever. But all claimed the right to sit with him and eat with him, and whoever wished insulted him without restraint; for no men in the world are less bound by convention or more unstable than the Eruli. Now when the evil deed had been accomplished, they were immediately repentant. For they said that they were not able to live without a ruler and without a general; so after much deliberation it seemed to them best in every way to summon one of their royal family from the island of Thule. And the reason for this I shall now explain. [415]

FOOTNOTES:

[188] Cf. Book IV. iv. 30.

[189] Modern Danube.

[190] Cf. Book III. ii. 2-6, VII. xxiv. 10.

[191] Book VII. xxxiv. 42.

XV

When the Eruli, being defeated by the Lombards in the above-mentioned battle, migrated from their ancestral homes, some of them, as has been told by me above,[192] made their home in the country of Illyricum, but the rest were averse to crossing the Ister River, but settled at the very extremity of the world; at any rate, these men, led by many of the royal blood, traversed all the nations of the Sclaveni one after the other, and after next crossing a large tract of barren country, they came to the Varni,[193] as they are called. After these they passed by the nations of the Dani,[194] without suffering violence at the hands of the barbarians there. Coming thence to the ocean, they took to the sea, and putting in at Thule,[195] remained there on the island.

Now Thule is exceedingly large; for it is more than ten times greater than Britain. And it lies far distant from it toward the north. On this island the land is for the most part barren, but in the inhabited country thirteen very numerous nations are settled; and there are kings over each nation. In that place a very wonderful thing takes [417]place each year. For the sun at the time of the summer solstice never sets for forty days, but appears constantly during this whole time above the earth. But not less than six months later, at about the time of the winter solstice, the sun is never seen on this island for forty days, but never-ending night envelops it; and as a result of this dejection holds the people there during this whole time, because they are unable by any means to mingle with one another during this interval. And although I was eager to go to this island and become an eye-witness of the things I have told, no opportunity ever presented itself. However, I made enquiry from those who come to us from the island as to how in the world they are able to reckon the length of the days, since the sun never rises nor sets there at the appointed times. And they gave me an account which is true and trustworthy. For they said that the sun during those forty days does not indeed set just as has been stated, but is visible to the people there at one time toward the east, and again toward the west.

Whenever, therefore, on its return, it reaches the same place on the horizon where they had previously been accustomed to see it rise, they reckon in this way that one day and night have passed. When, however, the time of the nights arrives, they always take note of the courses of the moon and stars and thus reckon the measure of the days. And when a time amounting to thirty-five [419]days has passed in this long night, certain men are sent to the summits of the mountains—for this is the custom among them—and when they are able from that point barely to see the sun, they bring back word to the people below that within five days the sun will shine upon them. And the whole population celebrates a festival at the good news, and that too in the darkness. And this is the greatest festival which the natives of Thule have; for, I imagine, these islanders always become terrified, although they see the same thing happen every year, fearing that the sun may at some time fail them entirely.

But among the barbarians who are settled in Thule, one nation only, who are called the Scrithiphini, live a kind of life akin to that of the beasts. For they neither wear garments of cloth nor do they walk with shoes on their feet, nor do they drink wine nor derive anything edible from the earth. For they neither till the land themselves, nor do their women work it for them, but the women regularly join the men in hunting, which is their only pursuit. For the forests, which are exceedingly large, produce for them a great abundance of wild beasts and other animals, as do also the mountains which rise there. And they feed exclusively upon the flesh of the wild beasts slain by them, and clothe themselves in their skins, and since they have neither flax nor any implement with which to sew, they fasten these skins together by the sinews of the animals, and in this way manage to cover the whole body. And indeed not even their infants are nursed in the same way as among the rest of mankind. For the children of the Scrithiphini do not feed upon the milk of women nor do they touch their mother's breast, but they are nourished upon [421]the marrow of the animals killed in the hunt, and upon this alone. Now as soon as a woman gives birth to a child, she throws it into a skin and straightway hangs it to a tree, and after putting marrow into its mouth she immediately sets out with her husband for the customary hunt. For they do everything in common and likewise engage in this pursuit together. So much for the daily life of these barbarians.

But all the other inhabitants of Thule, practically speaking, do not differ very much from the rest of men, but they reverence in great numbers gods and demons both of the heavens and of the air, of the earth and of the sea, and sundry other demons which are said to be in the waters of springs and rivers. And they incessantly offer up all kinds of sacrifices, and make oblations to the dead, but the noblest of sacrifices, in their eyes, is the first human being whom they have taken captive in war; for they sacrifice him to Ares, whom they regard as the greatest god. And the manner in which they offer up the captive is not by sacrificing him on an altar only, but also by hanging him to a tree, or throwing him among thorns, or killing him by some of the other most cruel forms of death. Thus, then, do the inhabitants of Thule live. And one of their most numerous nations is the Gauti, and it was next to them that the incoming Eruli settled at the time in question.

On the present occasion,[196] therefore, the Eruli who dwelt among the Romans, after the murder of their king had been perpetrated by them, sent some of [423]their notables to the island of Thule to search out and bring back whomsoever they were able to find there of the royal blood. And when these men reached the island, they found many there of the royal blood, but they selected the one man who pleased them most and set out with him on the return journey. But this man fell sick and died when he had come to the country of the Dani. These men therefore went a second time to the island and secured another man, Datius by name. And he was followed by his brother Aordus and two hundred youths of the Eruli in Thule. But since much time passed while they were absent on this journey, it occurred to the Eruli in the neighbourhood of Singidunum that they were not consulting their own interests in importing a leader from Thule against the wishes of the Emperor Justinian. They therefore sent envoys to Byzantium, begging the emperor to send them a ruler of his own choice. And he straightway sent them one of the Eruli who had long been sojourning in Byzantium, Suartuas by name. At first the Eruli welcomed him and did obeisance to him and rendered the customary obedience to his commands; but not many days later a messenger arrived with the tidings that the men from the island of Thule were near at hand. And Suartuas commanded them to go out to meet those men, his intention being to destroy them, and the Eruli, approving his purpose, immediately went with him. But when the two forces were one day's journey distant from each other, the king's men all abandoned him at night and went over of their own accord to the newcomers, while he himself took to flight and set out unattended for Byzantium. There[425]upon the emperor earnestly undertook with all his power to restore him to his office, and the Eruli, fearing the power of the Romans, decided to submit themselves to the Gepaedes. This, then, was the cause of the revolt of the Eruli.[197]

FOOTNOTES:

[192] This has not been stated before by Procopius.

[193] Or Varini, a tribe living on the coast near the mouth of the Rhine.

[194] A group of tribes inhabiting the Danish Peninsula.

[195] Probably Iceland or the northern portion of the Scandinavian peninsula, which was then regarded as an island and called "Scanza." The name of Thule was familiar from earlier times. It was described by the navigator Pytheas in the age of Alexander the Great, and he claimed to have visited the island. It was variously placed, but always considered the northernmost land in the world—"ultima Thule."

[196] Cf. Chap. xiv. 42.

[197] Chap. xiv. 37 introduces this topic.

Transcriber's Note: This text is a translation from the original Greek. The index in this original was linked by verse number and not page number. Due to translation contraints, not every verse translated directly. While every attempt has been made to make this index useful in the html version, some discrepancies of location by a few lines may occur.

This side by side translation is additionally the reason for the absence of even-numbered pages.

INDEX

Transcriber's Notes:

Obvious punctuation errors repaired.

Index:

The following words were changed so that the index matched what was actually in the text.

Original Index	Changed To
"Aclyinus"	"Aquilinus"
"Aegypt"	"Egypt"
"Peter"	"Pastor" (under Asclepiodotus)
"Giselicus"	"Giselic" (under Alaric and Giselic)
"Aquilea"	"Aquileia"
"Bandalarius"	"Vandalarius" (under Vandalarius and Visandus)
"Chorsomantis"	"Chorsamantis"
"Diomed"	"Diomedes" (twice under Beneventus)
"Messina"	"Messana" (under Charybdis and Scylla)

"Chersonnesus"	"Chersonese"
"Rudolphus"	"Rodolophus" (under Lombards)
"Viselicus"	"Giselic" (under Visigoths)
"Uraias"	"Uraïas"

Body-guard used four times in the A section in index changed to bodyguard to conform to text.

The remaining corrections made are indicated by dotted lines under the corrections. Scroll the mouse over the word and the original text will appear.

Im TheStory
personalised classic books
UNIQUE GIFT
FOR KIDS, PARTNERS AND FRIENDS
Timeless books such as:
Kids
Alice in Wonderland • The Jungle Book • The Wonderful Wizard of Oz
Peter and Wendy • Robin Hood • The Prince and The Pauper
The Railway Children • Treasure Island • A Christmas Carol
Adults
Romeo and Juliet • Dracula
Highly Customizable
Change Books Title
Replace
Upload
Add Inscriptions
Visit
ImTheStory.com
and order yours today!

Lightning Source UK Ltd.
Milton Keynes UK
UKHW02f0626150218
317932UK00008B/540/P